JEWS WITHOUT JUDAISM

D1002764

JEWS WITHOUT JUDAISM

*Conversations
with an
Unconventional
Rabbi*

Rabbi **Daniel Friedman**

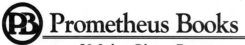

Prometheus Books

59 John Glenn Drive
Amherst, New York 14228-2197

Published 2002 by Prometheus Books

Jews without Judaism: Conversations with an Unconventional Rabbi. Copyright © 2002 by Rabbi Daniel Friedman. All rights reserved. No part of this publication may be reproduced, stored in a retrieval system, or transmitted in any form or by any means, digital, electronic, mechanical, photocopying, recording, or otherwise, or conveyed via the Internet or a Web site without prior written permission of the publisher, except in the case of brief quotations embodied in critical articles and reviews.

Inquiries should be addressed to
Prometheus Books
59 John Glenn Drive
Amherst, New York 14228–2197
VOICE: 716–691–0133, ext. 207
FAX: 716–564–2711
WWW.PROMETHEUSBOOKS.COM

06 05 04 03 02   5 4 3 2 1

Library of Congress Cataloging-in-Publication Data pending

ISBN 1–57392–924–7

Printed in the United States of America on acid-free paper

My wife, Felice, has been my constant inspiration, encouragement, critic, and partner throughout this enterprise as she has for the forty-five years of our marriage. If this book has any value, it is due, in no small measure, to the countless discussions we have had and to her persistence in pursuing truth, even unto its innermost parts.

Contents

PREFACE

About the Conversations

Over the course of my forty years as a congregational rabbi, I have engaged in thousands of conversations about the existence of God, the meaning of being Jewish, the causes and consequences of inter-marriage, and the nature and significance of anti-Semitism—all matters of great concern to many Jews, whatever their religious beliefs. Each of the following "fictional" conversations represents the distillation of dozens, in some cases hundreds, of actual conversations on these issues. Together, they are intended to convey an understanding of Judaism and Jews that is not available in conventional treatments of either.

I do not claim that I am a typical rabbi. While still in seminary (the Hebrew Union College, where I was ordained in 1962), I came to a number of unconventional conclusions about Judaism that have been confirmed and refined over the years. Rather than set them forth here, I leave them for the reader to discover as the conversations unfold. The first chapter is a brief essay in which I present, in more formal terms, my thesis that Judaism, the religion, has ended, while Jews, the people, con-tinue. I realize that this is not what rabbis are "supposed" to say. It is time, though, for someone to reveal that the emperor is naked. It is time for Jews to be honest about themselves and their Jewishness. They have nothing to lose but confusion and guilt.

Introduction

Americans Jews are the luckiest Jews in history. They live in a place and time that offer far more freedom, opportunity, and security than Jews have ever known. In every field of endeavor—intellectual, commercial, cultural, political—the number of prominent Jews far exceeds their proportion (2.3 percent) of the general population.[1] That Jews are no longer considered a minority[2] indicates the extent to which they have succeeded in becoming, and have been accepted as, part of the mainstream population. It is no exaggeration to assert that the best thing that ever happened to the Jews is the United States of America.

Ironically, at the very time and in the very place that the achievements of Jews have reached unprecedented heights, most students of the American Jewish community predict and agonize over its demise. One can hardly find an article or book concerning American Jews that does not refer to the "crisis" confronting the community:

"Today, almost everything is possible for individual American Jews, but the outlook is bleak for the future of American Jewry as a community."[3]

"After nearly four centuries, the momentum of Jewish experience in America is essentially spent. . . . [Without a spiritual revival] American Jewish history will soon end, and become a part of American memory as a whole."[4]

"Saving an unforeseen reversal of current trends, it appears from the

11

present perspective that the history of the Jews as we have known it and them is probably approaching the end."[5]

"The Jewish people as a whole, as an ethnic entity, is threatened with erosion and communal extinction. What the Holocaust began physically will, in the twenty-first century, be accomplished culturally."[6]

"It is because of its very virtues that America is in danger of becoming the most luxurious burial ground ever of Jewish cultural existence."[7]

"American Jewish life is in danger of disappearing, just as most American Jews have achieved everything we ever wanted: acceptance, influence, affluence, equality."[8]

It may fairly be said that religion plays virtually no part in the lives of most American Jews.[9] In our time, a phenomenon never previously in evidence has emerged: vast numbers of Jews without Judaism. Although there may have been, in other times and in other places, individual Jews who abandoned their religion and yet remained Jews, today more Jews are secular than religious. They may "observe" a few of the rituals of Judaism, celebrating, albeit in the most minimal fashion, a Jewish holiday here and there, perhaps lighting Chanukah candles and participating in a seder at Passover.[10] They may even belong to synagogues and temples, enroll their children in religious schools, celebrate a bar or bat mitzvah, engage rabbis to officiate at their weddings and funerals. But in their daily lives, the beliefs and requirements of Judaism have no bearing upon their decisions.[11] Their diet, dress, interpersonal relationships, and choice of occupation and spouse are not regulated or influenced by Judaism—not by biblical, Talmudic, or *halachic* principles—but by the same secular concerns and values that motivate non-Jewish Americans. Whereas all Jewish behavior was once deemed subject to divine authority as expressed in sacred texts and the laws articulated therein, today, none is.

Furthermore, what little religious behavior remains in the lives of American Jews is motivated largely by a secular, not a religious, rationale: maintaining one's connection to other Jews, providing opportunities for family togetherness, and inculcating in one's children an awareness of their Jewishness—rather than fulfilling commandments. Services are attended, if at all, not for the purpose of divine worship, but in order to renew one's membership in the Jewish people on certain unofficially mandated, community-wide celebrations of Jewishness, such as Rosh Hashanah and Yom Kippur. Children are educated, not so that they will know what their Creator requires of them, but so that they will know they are Jewish. Being Jewish is important; being religious is not.

Many Jews wonder whether they are really Jewish after all. Having been taught that being Jewish means being part of a *religious* community, they ask themselves if they truly qualify. Can one be Jewish without God? Without religion? Without Judaism?

Such are the questions to be considered in the following pages. In the course of offering answers to these questions, it will become clear that an important distinction must be made between *Jewish identity*, a social-historical-cultural-ethnic matter, and *Judaism*, the system of beliefs and practices properly considered a religion. It is my contention that Judaism, the religion, came to an end some two hundred years ago; that subsequent "Judaisms" (Reform, Conservative, Reconstructionist, Humanistic, and, to some extent, even Orthodox) are, in fact, not religions but secularized modifications of Judaism; and that, aside from a relatively small number of sincerely committed believers and practitioners of Halachic Judaism,* Jews have, in effect, said farewell to Judaism.

NOTES

1. "Jews comprise over a third of the billionaires in this country, over a quarter of the multi-millionaires, and between a third and a half of the elite professionals in law, in journalism, in medicine, and in academia." Steven M. Cohen, "Undue Stress on American Anti-Semitism?" *Sh'ma* 19, no. 376 (September 1, 1989): 113. Many of America's elite universities, which at one time limited severely the number of Jewish students they admitted, now have Jewish *presidents*. For example, at the time of this writing, the presidents of Princeton, Yale, Harvard, and Northwestern universities are Jews. More than one-third of America's Nobel Prize winners have been Jews. Jews occupy a disproportionate number of seats in Congress (37) and on the Supreme Court (2). The Federal Reserve Board's chairman, one of the nation's most powerful positions, is a Jew, and he has served in this capacity for four consecutive terms, under presidents of both parties. If there were yet any doubt that the Jews are "at home" in

---

*Halachic Judaism is described in the next chapter, note 1.

America, the nomination of Joseph Lieberman for the office of vice-president of the United States puts that doubt to rest.

2. "In the new lexicon of American ethnicity Jews no longer constitute a minority group, notwithstanding the fact that they represent only 2.5 percent of the American population. Minority status is now limited to those who continue to be handicapped by past or present discrimination. On these criteria, Jews now belong to the advantaged majority." Charles E. Silberman, *A Certain People: American Jews and Their Lives Today* (New York: Summit, 1985), p. 82.

3. Seymour P. Lachman and Barry A. Kosmin, "What Is Happening to American Jewry?" *New York Times*, June 4, 1990.

4. Arthur Hertzberg, *The Jews in America: Four Centuries of an Uneasy Encounter* (New York: Simon and Schuster, 1989), pp. 386–88.

5. Norman F. Cantor, *The Sacred Chain: A History of the Jews* (New York: HarperCollins, 1994), p. 425.

6. Ibid., p. 437.

7. Ari Shavit, "Vanishing," *New York Times Magazine* (June 8, 1997).

8. Alan M. Dershowitz, *The Vanishing American Jew* (Boston: Little, Brown and Company, 1997), p. 1.

9. ". . . [R]elatively few American Jews still believe in a God who makes demands upon them; even fewer regard those demands as binding." Silberman, *A Certain People*, p. 160.

10. "For many American Jews, attending a seder or lighting Chanukah candles is an ethnic far more than a religious act; it is a way of asserting cultural and national identity rather than of obeying God's law. . . . Secular Jews are turning to religious rituals to affirm their Jewish identity." Silberman, *A Certain People*, p. 235.

11. "Outside of segregationist-Orthodoxy which forms less than 10 percent of the numbers of American Jewry (a smaller proportion of American Jews than those who celebrate Christmas by going to Church) the regnant ideas that animate American Jews and explain to them who they are and what they must do in no way exhibit the traits common among religious ideas and attitudes. Most American Jews do not do the things Judaism says Judaist-Jews should do. . . . Proportions of those who identify with Judaism and actually practice the faith prove negligible, except on a few distinctive occasions." Jacob Neusner, *Jewish Spectator* (winter 1994–95): 26.

The Judaism That Is No More[1]

J udaism ended some two to three centuries ago with the arrival of modernity—that is, with the Enlightenment and Emancipation; the rise of modern science and the Industrial Revolution; the emergence of democracy, equality, and, perhaps above all, when reason replaced faith as the dominant mode of truth seeking in the Western world. Together, these powerful forces created a new understanding of humanity and the universe. No longer viewed as the helpless pawn of supernatural forces, humanity achieved an unprecedented sense of power and dignity as the species able to understand aspects of reality previously unexplored and thereby able to control what was hitherto beyond control. Modernity undermined Judaism's basic assumptions and rendered it obsolete.

It is important to review the Judaism that is no more in order to understand clearly the present condition of the Jews and of Judaism. Judaism begins, in the biblical text, with a belief about the Jewish people: The Jews were created by the divine decision that they are a special people whose purpose is to obey the divine commandments (*mitzvot*) as they are revealed in the holy Torah,* and to bring the truth of God's revelation to the rest of humanity. This concept of the Chosen People (*am segulah*) is central to the biblical saga. It was on the basis of an agreement between Yahweh and his Chosen People that they were to know

---

*Torah—the handwritten parchment scroll consisting of the first five books of the Bible, traditionally believed to be God's revelation to Moses at Mt. Sinai.

15

themselves as a holy people (*am kadosh*), a people covenanted to act in certain specific ways that would make them distinctive. They were to be different from other peoples. Their diet was to be different. Their males were to be circumcised. They were to observe the Sabbath and other holy days and festivals. A host of additional prescriptions and prohibitions would separate them from other peoples and make them holy.

In return for upholding their part of the Covenant (i.e., in return for loyalty to Yahweh and obedience to his laws) various benefits would accrue to the Jewish people: a land of their own was promised to them; their enemies would be vanquished; their flocks and fields would be protected; they would prosper; their descendents would multiply. Both the purpose and value of the people, Israel, and of its commitment to Yahweh were thus clearly delineated in a text held to be divinely authored.

In the postbiblical rabbinic period, the time during which the Talmud and other major rabbinic works were written, the rabbis created the *halacha*, a vast and complex body of law that would govern the Jews for over a thousand years. The *halacha* greatly expanded the purpose and value of the Covenant. It was now the duty (and privilege) of every Jew to observe not merely the *mitzvot* contained in the Bible, but the much larger number of laws, the *halacha*, as ordained by rabbinic authorities. These laws, too, it was believed, were divinely authoritative. Virtually every one of an individual's acts and decisions thereby came under the authority of Jewish law, from the first words recited and the actions performed upon rising in the morning to those in the final moments of consciousness at night; from dress to diet; from the marital relationship to commercial activity. Included, of course, was the elaborate regimen of ritual activity governing the day, the week, the month, and the year. In return, the individual would earn God's blessings, his favor, and a benefit not included in the biblical Covenant—eternal life. The rabbis added bodily resurrection and life in the world to come as God's most precious gift to his loyal and obedient servants.

The individual's eternal destiny depended upon the extent to which one was faithful to the sacred law as it was meticulously articulated in holy books, the study of which was itself a sacred duty. Among life's most serious tasks was the mastery of the sacred texts in order that one would be fully aware of the prescribed and prohibited activities upon which one's salvation depended.

It is important to understand that Judaism comprised a doctrine not only about God, but about the Jewish people. It offered clear and cogent answers not only to the questions: What is God and what does he require of us? but: What does it mean to be a Jew and how does one fulfill one's responsibilities as a Jew? Judaism asserted that being Jewish offered benefits granted to no other people, and that Judaism required separating oneself from others and their false beliefs in order to demonstrate God's authenticity and the truth of his law.

Furthermore, Judaism may be seen as a justification for the plight of the Jews, a rationalization for their being in exile, an explanation for their ostracization and persecution. That is, Judaism answered the question that would weigh heavily on the people over the centuries: Why do the Jews suffer? The answer is reiterated in various rabbinic texts and throughout Jewish liturgy. Just as the Israelites were allowed to suffer for four hundred years as slaves in Egypt in order that Yahweh could demonstrate his might to the Egyptians; and just as the Israelites were taken through the wilderness of Sinai on their journey to the Promised Land so that Yahweh could prove to them their total dependence upon his grace and prove to other nations his extraordinary power to keep alive an entire nation in a desolate desert, so their current travails and all of history is preparation for the eventual and inevitable triumph of Yahweh's power in the "end of days," when all people will acknowledge his power and sovereignty. In the meantime, if Jews suffer, it is for two reasons: their suffering is caused by evil people and nations who have not yet acknowledged the truth of Yahweh and the holiness of his people; and it is the divine punishment brought upon all Jews for the failure of some to be loyal to his law.[2]

For fifteen centuries, Judaism was a cogent and compelling answer to questions of a powerless, subjugated, and homeless people. Judaism's answers required not only observance of a daily regimen of sanctified acts, but offered a comprehensive philosophy of life, providing answers to all questions about life's meaning and purpose. It set forth a complete theory of the value of Jewish existence. All this in addition to its rich calendar of holidays and festivals.

In the course of fulfilling the requirements of Judaism, of the *halacha*, the Jews created a distinctive culture (although it was not their conscious purpose to do so). Their food, clothing, language—not to mention their "religious" behavior—were different from other peoples'. That which we today consider Jewish culture was a by-product of Judaism, the result of the community's commitment to what it believed to be a sacred body of law that governed every aspect of life.

We must not overlook the fact that underlying every *halachically* required action and decision was a single and sufficient reason: because God commands it. I do this not because it will be spiritually uplifting, or because it will promote family or community solidarity, or because it will be good for my children, or because it will help the Jewish people survive, but because it is God's will that I behave in this way. It is both my sacred obligation and privilege to behave thus. I dare not, nor would I wish to, disobey God's sacred instructions.

This all-encompassing way of life came to an end approximately two hundred years ago. Today, in the aftermath of the Enlightenment and modernity, all but a tiny minority[3] of Jews stand outside its authority and influence. For the vast majority of Jews today, being Jewish has nothing to do with observing the *halacha*, and the rationale for being Jewish provided by Halachic Judaism is utterly unpersuasive. Today, Jews, by and large, do not experience themselves as a people in exile, as strangers in others' lands.[4] On the contrary, especially in the United States of America where the largest proportion of the world's Jewish population is concentrated, Jews increasingly feel "at home" in a culture that they have had a disproportionate role in creating. The Judaism of exile, suffering, and exclusion no longer speaks to them. It belongs to a different universe of belief.

Most Jews derive their actual beliefs about the universe, nature, life, death, interpersonal relationships, morality, and politics not from the Bible, the Talmud, or any Judaic text or source, but from popular culture, science, and philosophy.[5] They experience reality in secular, not religious, terms.

This is not to suggest that Jews are necessarily atheists. Some are, and some are not. The reason that so many Jews are estranged from Judaism is that even those who do believe in God no longer accept the classical definition of the Jews as the divinely chosen people whose sacred responsibility is to obey the *halacha*. Yet they continue to identify themselves as Jews. They wish to maintain their connection to the Jewish people and to the history of the Jewish people. They are proud of that history and see no reason to cut themselves apart from it.

Their pride explains the continuing need that many Jews in this postreligious age experience for synagogues—not as places of worship, but as educational and social centers where the history and meaning of Jewish identity and experience may be explored objectively[6] and celebrated (the modern purpose of Jewish holidays[7]). For the synagogue to be responsive to this need, it is necessary to see today's Jews neither as loyal inheritors nor as wayward betrayers of an ancient faith, but as they really are: contemporary members of an ancient people who no longer share the beliefs of their ancestors. They are Jews without Judaism.

NOTES

1. By "Judaism" I mean Halachic Judaism, the Judaism created by the rabbis who authored the Talmud and subsequent texts, and who thereby created the *halacha*, the body of authoritative law that governed the Jewish people from the second through the eighteenth centuries.

It is commonly and correctly understood that a religion is a body of distinctive beliefs, practices, and recommended behavior that serves to unite a community of persons who perceive their identity as members of the community as deriving from a common commitment to this body of distinctive beliefs, practices, and behavior. Christianity, Islam, Buddhism, and Halachic Judaism are examples of religions that conform to this understanding.

In asserting that Judaism came to an end with modernity, I mean to suggest that none of the subsequent "Judaisms"—Reform, Conservative, Reconstructionist, and Humanistic—truly qualifies as an authentic Judaism: as a distinctive, independent body of belief and practice. Rather, each consists of belief and practice taken, in part, from Halachic Judaism and, in part, from general, secular culture. All are derivative and imitative rather than original and independent. None offers a worldview of its own. None consists, as does Halachic Judaism, of a comprehensive and *distinctive* philosophy of life and of Jewish identity. None is articulated in a body of indigenous texts that are not themselves derived from either Halachic Judaism or from general, secular culture. Each denies (Reform, Reconstructionist, and Humanistic) or compromises (Conservative) the supernatural authority of the *halacha* and thereby voids the obligation to obey its requirements. Only Orthodox Judaism demands commitment to that authority, and may thereby be considered an authentic Judaism.

2. This belief causes many modern Jews embarrassment. When the chief

rabbi of Israel asserted that the Holocaust was divine punishment visited upon the Jews for their sins, many Jews were outraged. However, this assertion is consistent with classical Judaism's theory of Jewish suffering.

3. That is, those within the Orthodox community who continue to believe themselves obligated to fulfill the requirements of the *halacha*.

4. The large majority choose not to live in the State of Israel although they are free to do so. For many Jews, the very concept of exile—central to Halachic Judaism—is of no significance.

5. Some may claim to base their behavior on the Ten Commandments or on other "Jewish teachings," but most can name no more than a few of the commandments, and fewer can elucidate in any but the most superficial terms what those teachings are. As Daniel Gordis, Dean of Administration at the University of Judaism in Los Angeles, writes: "Even those commitments which we claim are a result of our Jewish tradition are merely liberal commitments dressed in Jewish garb and vocabulary. . . . American Jews know (though they are hesitant to admit it) that their values and ideals are defined not by Judaism but by American liberalism; Judaism provides only an ethnic vocabulary for expressing the values they have already adopted. In the end, that renders Judaism irrelevant." "The End of Survivalist Judaism? American Jews in Search of Direction," *Sh'ma* 24, no. 466 (January 21, 1994): 6.

6. With a view toward understanding the actual, rather than legendary or mythological, origins and evolution of the Jewish people, utilizing the best results of modern scholarship.

7. That is, as expressions of such humanistic values as freedom, independence, peace, courage, love, and integrity, rather than as rituals of devotion to a benevolent, supernatural deity.

CONVERSATION
ONE

Intermarriage

Steve: Hello, Rabbi, I'm Steve and this is my fiancée, Christine.

Rabbi: Hello. I understand you are planning a wedding.

Steve: Yes, and we're hoping you will officiate.

Chris: Because I'm not Jewish, but we were told you officiate at interfaith ceremonies.

Rabbi: I'm curious. Why do you want a rabbi to officiate?

Steve: To tell you the truth, Rabbi, I'm not very religious. I'm doing this for my parents. They would have a fit if we were married by a priest.

Rabbi: Do they object to your marriage?

Steve: Not at all. They love Chris. They just want a Jewish wedding.

Rabbi: And how do you feel about it, Chris?

Chris: I like the idea. We attended a Jewish wedding a few weeks
                ago and it was nice. Actually, I am more religious than
                Steve. I go to church occasionally. He never goes to temple.

Steve: Like I said, I'm not very religious. But being Jewish is very
                important to me. I don't need to go to services to be Jewish.
                I believe in God and I believe in being a good person. Isn't
                that what being Jewish is all about, Rabbi?

Rabbi: How about you, Chris? Do you believe in God and in being
                a good person?

Chris: Sure. I keep telling Steve: There's more to being Jewish
                than that. If that were all there is to it, I'd be Jewish, too,
                and I'm not.

Rabbi: Chris, what more is there to being Jewish, in your opinion?

Chris: Well, Steve's family's rabbi told us you have to go temple
                and observe the holidays and bring up your children as
                Jews.

Rabbi: And you don't agree, Steve?

Steve: No. None of my Jewish friends go to temple. The most any
                of us ever do is have a seder* or go to services on Yom
                Kippur.† Sure, I want my children to be Jewish. But I don't
                care if they're not religious.

Rabbi: Tell me, Chris, do you believe in Christ?

Chris: I guess so.

---

*Seder—the home ceremony held on Passover, consisting of an elaborate ritual feast during
which the legendary Exodus from Egypt is recounted and distinctive foods, symbols, and songs dra-
matize the significance of freedom to all peoples in all times.

†Yom Kippur—the Day of Atonement when, traditionally, Jews seek forgiveness for sins committed during the previous year.

Steve:　　You *do?*

Chris:　　Sure. You knew that.

Steve:　　I did *not.* You never told me.

Chris:　　You knew I'm Christian.

Steve:　　I just thought that means you believe in God.

Rabbi:　　Chris, is it important to you that your children believe in Christ? That they be baptized?

Chris:　　I would like it. But I'm willing to have them be Jewish if that's what Steve wants.

Rabbi:　　Steve, how would you feel about your children being Christian?

Steve:　　No way! I thought we agreed that they wouldn't.

Chris:　　We never really talked about it. You never want to talk about religion.

Steve:　　I'm just not interested. All I want is to have a rabbi marry us.

THREE WEEKS LATER

Rabbi:　　It's good to see you again. Have you been thinking about our last conversation?

Steve:　　Yes, and we read the book you recommended. The book about intermarriage.

Chris: It was the first time we ever really talked about religion. And about our children and how we want to raise them.

Rabbi: Did you come to any conclusions?

Steve: I think so. We agreed that Chris doesn't have to convert, but that our children will be Jewish.

Chris: That's right. But I'm still confused. I can't understand why it's so important to Steve that his children be Jewish if he doesn't even go to temple himself. He doesn't pray to God. He doesn't observe the Sabbath. He has no interest in the Jewish religion, yet he insists that his children be Jewish.

Steve: I keep telling her, Judaism isn't like Christianity. You don't have to believe or do anything to be Jewish. You just are.

Rabbi: Steve, how did you get to be Jewish?

Steve: I was born Jewish.

Rabbi: Chris, how did you get to be Christian?

Chris: My parents had me baptized.

Rabbi: Was that all?

Chris: And then, when I was older, I was confirmed.

Rabbi: Meaning . . .

Chris: I confirmed that I believed in Christ and wanted to be a Christian.

Rabbi: Steve, did you ever decide to be Jewish? Did you ever go through a ceremony that made you a Jew or that confirmed your Jewishness.

Steve: Not really. I had a *b'ris** and a bar mitzvah.† But I was
            Jewish anyway.

Rabbi: Correct. Even according to Orthodox Judaism, if a person's
            mother is Jewish, he or she is Jewish. No ceremony, no
            decision. So, Steve is correct: one does not have to believe
            or do anything to be Jewish. Birth determines it.

Chris: Then why call it a religion? A religion means you have cer-
            tain beliefs, doesn't it?

Rabbi: You've just put your finger on one of the most important
            things to understand about being Jewish: It's not a religious
            identity. Judaism is a religion, but not all Jews are religious.

Chris: You said it's not a religious identity. Then what is it?

Rabbi: It's hard to find words that accurately describe what being
            Jewish means. It has to do with a sense of being part of a long
            history; of being part of a people, the Jewish people, that is
            like an extended family with "branches" all over the world
            and reaching back many centuries into the past. It means
            feeling connected to other Jews, even though one may not
            speak their language or even agree with their religious beliefs.

Steve: That's it. When I say I'm not religious I don't mean I'm not
            Jewish. Being Jewish is very important to me, but I don't
            have to go to services or keep kosher.‡ It's something here,
            in my gut.

---

*B'ris (or *b'rit*)—the ritual circumcision traditionally performed on all Jewish males on the
eighth day after birth. The ceremony, during which the child is formally named, recalls the biblical
Abraham's circumcision whereby he entered into the covenant (*b'ris* or *b'rit*) with his God.

    †Bar mitzvah—literally, "son of the commandment"—the coming-of-age ceremony whereby
the thirteen-year-old boy (for girls, *bat* mitzvah) is inducted into the adult community and is there-
after responsible for fulfilling the commandments of Judaism.

    ‡To keep kosher—observing the halachically required dietary laws, which specify the animals,
birds, and fish that may be consumed and how they are to be slaughtered and prepared. The Hebrew
kosher means "fit" or "proper."

Rabbi: You're not the only one. As a matter of fact, today most Jews are not religious. They may observe a Jewish holiday once in a while, although even when they do, it's more to express their Jewishness—their membership in the Jewish people—than to "practice" Judaism. They may even belong to a synagogue or temple—again, more to connect with other Jews than to worship.

Chris: Are you saying a person can be a nonreligious Jew?

Rabbi: Most Jews are. They are secular Jews. I realize this sounds strange to a Christian. Christianity is a religion, with a specific set of beliefs that all Christians share. It's the belief in Christ that makes them all Christians. There is no comparable belief that all Jews share. You've probably heard the old joke: If you have two Jews, you have three opinions. Being Jewish is like having friends who grew up in the same neighborhood but are now scattered throughout the world. They share common memories and history, but they may have grown in different directions and come to different conclusions about the meaning of their experience as Jews—about the meaning of life itself. There is no single Jewish belief about anything. Including God. Many Jews do not believe in God, although most people assume that to be Jewish is to be religious and to be religious is, at the very least, to believe in God.

Chris: Why don't they believe in God?

Rabbi: We'll take up that question next time. The answer requires an understanding of Jewish experience that we haven't yet touched upon. I think you'll find that this understanding explains a good deal of what otherwise appears to be a mystery about the Jewish people. It will also help explain why many Jews have a problem believing in God.

THREE WEEKS LATER

Steve: Rabbi, I think you helped clear up something I've been bothered about for a long time.

Rabbi: What is that?

Steve: When we first met you, I told you I believed in God. To tell you the truth, I only said that because I thought you would expect me to. I thought I had to say I believe in God in order to be Jewish. Now I realize that I don't really believe in God, but I'm still Jewish. I think lots of Jews think they believe in God, or pretend to, just so that they will be Jewish. But when you see that being Jewish doesn't require believing in God, you can be more honest. Now I realize that I haven't believed in God since I was a little child. Maybe even then I wasn't sure. When my grandfather died, my aunt told me God took him for reasons we can't understand. That really upset me. When my grandfather was in the hospital, I prayed to God to make him better. And he died. When the rabbi came to the house, he said something to me—I don't remember what—but I do remember asking him why God took my grandfather when I had prayed for him to get well. The rabbi said God doesn't always do what we ask, and I think that was the moment I began to doubt that there really is a God.

Rabbi: It's interesting that you should bring this up, because it is exactly what I want to discuss with you today. You see, Jewish history is very much like the experience you had as a child. For centuries, Jews prayed that God would save them from their enemies—from the persecution they suffered time and again, in country after country, ever since they were expelled from their own land two thousand years ago. Finally, in our own century, during my lifetime, the greatest tragedy ever to occur in Jewish history, the

Holocaust, wiped out one-third of the Jewish people. And do you know which Jews bore the brunt of the slaughter? The believers. The most traditional of Jews. Where was God? How could he allow such a catastrophe?

Steve: I've asked this myself, but I was always told that it wasn't God's fault. That he created human beings with the power to do good or evil and he can't control them when they do evil.

Rabbi: Then why pray? If God is not able to protect his own, "chosen" people, what is the purpose of praying for anything? I have found that Jews, by and large, have learned from their own experience and from Jewish experience that prayer does not work.

Chris: When I pray, it's not to ask for anything from God but to say what's on my mind.

Steve: I don't understand why you need God for that.

Chris: It helps to know that someone is listening.

Steve: Does it matter that someone is listening if there is no answer?

Rabbi: For many Jews, prayer and the concept of a God to whom one prays are no longer meaningful. They don't necessarily come right out and deny that there is a God. Perhaps, like you, Steve, they think they "have" to believe in God in order to be Jewish, so they pretend to believe what, in fact, they do not truly believe. But that belief is empty. It's just words.

Steve: You've just described my whole family. They say they believe in God, in the Torah, in Judaism, but they really don't. They don't even know what is in the Torah. They don't study it. They have never read it!

Chris: It's true. I know more about the Bible than Steve's parents do. But whenever we talk about religion or God or being Jewish, it's as though they aren't really listening to me.

Steve: She's right. My parents—Jews, in general—don't care what Christians have to say.

Rabbi: Now we're getting into another difficult area. Many Jews associate Christianity with anti-Semitism. So much of Jewish history includes the pain of being persecuted—often at the hands of Christians who accused the Jews of responsibility for the crucifixion of Jesus and who punished them for this "crime." It's difficult for Jews to believe this evil accusation and the Jewish suffering it brought have ended. Older Jews especially, people who experienced anti-Semitism themselves in their childhood or in their adult lives, can't trust that anti-Semitism has declined and almost vanished from the scene, at least here in America. They continue to be very sensitive to the least bit of evidence, or what appears to be evidence, of anti-Semitism. And they are especially suspicious of Christianity, given the long history of anti-Jewish feeling among Christians.

Chris: This really surprises me. I realize that Christians used to say terrible things about the Jews. But that was so long ago. I've never heard anything against the Jews. My priest says we should love the Jews. They are the people of our Lord. I can't believe Jews think that Christians hate them.

Rabbi: We're talking about certain people with deep-seated feelings, fears that possibly are unconscious. Even though most present-day Christians may have no anti-Semitic feelings at all, and even if the church condemns anti-Semitism, not all Jews have been able to overcome centuries of teachings to the contrary. And this explains why some Jews find intermarriage so difficult to accept. They feel that an "enemy" is entering the family.

Chris: That's exactly what I felt they were thinking! Not your par-
              ents, exactly, Steve. But some of your other relatives. It was
              as though I were trying to break into this special family and
              ruin it!

Steve: But they love you!

Rabbi: Remember, what may be going on is not necessarily all on
              a conscious level. They may very well love Chris. But deep
              down, they may still feel that somehow her presence in the
              family is a betrayal.

Steve: Betrayal?

Rabbi: Of those centuries of Jewish suffering at the hands of "her
              people."

Steve: I guess you have a point. That would explain why my family
              is so adamant about not having the wedding in her church.

Rabbi: For Christians, the church is the ideal place for a wedding.
              It has positive associations for them. The cross is a positive
              symbol. For Jews, the cross represents Jewish suffering. It
              reminds them of the church which, for centuries, perse-
              cuted them. And for one's own son or daughter to be mar-
              ried in such a place is the ultimate betrayal of Jewish his-
              tory—even though the Jewish people involved may not be
              at all religious.

Chris: I see that being Jewish is a lot more complicated than I
              thought.

CONVERSATION TWO

Jews without Judaism

Jerry: I wanted to talk to you, Rabbi, because when you mentioned your Orthodox background in your sermon last Saturday, I realized we have a lot in common and I thought you could help me with something I'm confused about. When I was a child, I, too, went to shul* every Shabbos.† I was really religious as a kid.

Rabbi: What do you mean by "religious"?

Jerry: I mean going to services, keeping kosher, not riding on Shabbos‡ . . .

Rabbi: Do you recall *why* you did those things?

Jerry: That's the way I was brought up.

Rabbi: Your family did them.

Jerry: Everyone—my family, friends, neighbors . . .

---

*Shul—the Yiddish word for synagogue.
†Sabbath.
‡According to Halachic Judaism, riding, even to the synagogue, is a form of work, which is prohibited on the Sabbath.

Rabbi: You simply followed their example.

Jerry: Yes. We kept kosher, went to shul every week . . .

Rabbi: Did you consider, as a child, *not* doing these things?

Jerry: Not really. You were Jewish, you did them.

Rabbi: So, being Jewish was the *reason* behind these "religious" activities?

Jerry: Sure.

Rabbi: But today, you do none of them? Is that right?

Jerry: Almost none.

Rabbi: Are you still Jewish?

Jerry: Yes, but this is where I'm confused, Rabbi. I still feel just as Jewish as when I was religious.

Rabbi: What do you mean, you "feel Jewish"?

Jerry: It's my history, my people, my heritage.

Rabbi: And your religion?

Jerry: Well, I guess you could say there are different ways to be Jewish.

Rabbi: Religious and nonreligious?

Jerry: Right.

Rabbi: Suppose you had been brought up without any religious examples: no shul, no keeping kosher. Would you still have been Jewish?

Jerry: Of course. Some of my best friends were like that.

Rabbi: Jews without Judaism?

Jerry: I never really thought about it that way, but yes, Jewish without Judaism.

Rabbi: And you? What are you today?

Jerry: Well, I still light candles on Shabbos—sometimes. We have a seder. Chanukah candles. I guess I'm still somewhat religious, just not as much as when I was a child.

Rabbi: I wonder, though, *why* you do even these few things. Is it because you believe in God?

Jerry: No. I'm not even sure I believe in God. I do them because I'm Jewish.

Rabbi: So, lighting candles is your way of expressing your Jewishness?

Jerry: Exactly.

Rabbi: But not necessary.

Jerry: Necessary?

Rabbi: You're saying it isn't necessary to light candles or keep kosher or attend services in order to be Jewish.

Jerry: Right. It isn't necessary. But it helps. You know, you feel more Jewish when you do these things.

Rabbi: Not more religious?

Jerry: Not really.

Rabbi: There is a difference, then, between Jewishness and Judaism? Between, as you put it, feeling part of Jewish history, part of the Jewish people; and being part of Judaism—worshiping God?

Jerry: There must be. As I said, I'm not sure I even believe in God. But I am sure I'm Jewish.

Rabbi: And when you light candles or perform other "religious" activities, you are really doing so not as a religious act but as a social act?

Jerry: I'm not sure what you mean by "social."

Rabbi: In the sense that you are acting so as to connect with other Jews. It is the Jewish people, rather than God, that you have in mind when you light candles.

Jerry: Or when I go to shul. To tell you the truth, I don't really go to pray to God. I go to be with my people. I mean, with my people past *and* present.

Rabbi: What you are saying is true for most Jews today. They participate in what used to be religious activities for nonreligious reasons: in order to feel part of the Jewish people, in order to help preserve the Jewish people. These are secular, not religious, reasons. My grandfather kept kosher because he believed God commanded him to do so. He prayed to God three times every day—not in order to be with other Jews in the synagogue, although that was a secondary benefit, but because he believed that God required it of him.

Jerry: So, when I go to shul on the High Holidays,* I'm going for secular reasons?

Rabbi: Most Jews do. After all, why don't they go every week, every day? If they truly are religious, they would. The fact that most of them go only on the High Holidays indicates that their motivation is other than religious. They go because going to the synagogue on those two days each year has become, in our time and place, the way Jews "renew" their membership in the Jewish people. It's like an annual convention.

Jerry: That would explain a lot of things, Rabbi. For example, every Yom Kippur, my childhood rabbi used to scold the congregation for not coming to services. "All year," he would say, "you stay away. Why, on just this one day, are you here? The prayers are the same as they were last week when only fifteen people were here. Today there are eight hundred!" I always thought it was strange that he would use this one occasion when they *were* there to tell them that they should be there more often.

Rabbi: But he was correct, if you look at Jewish behavior as the expression of religious belief. If, on the other hand, you realize that we are no longer religious and that the synagogue itself has become a secular institution, then it makes sense that Jews come together on the High Holidays, not to pray, but to be with one another.

Jerry: But why bother? Why do we take the trouble to be Jewish, if we are no longer religious?

---

*Or, High Holy Days—Rosh Hashanah (New Year Day) and Yom Kippur (Day of Atonement), the two holidays celebrated in the fall.

A WEEK LATER

Rabbi: Last week we were making the distinction between being Jewish as a social experience or identity, and Judaism as a religion, a system of belief and practice ordained by God. You asked why Jews continue being Jewish if the religion is not important to us.

Jerry: Hasn't being Jewish always gone hand in hand with being religious? If you eliminate the religion, what's the point in being Jewish?

Rabbi: Let me back up a bit. Only very recently has it even been possible to separate the two. Prior to the seventeenth or eighteenth century, there was no distinction in the minds of Jews between religion and the rest of life. There was not even a word for "religion." Nor was there a word for "Judaism." Being a Jew was to be part of God's holy people. It was to be bound by the covenant between God and his people. It was to be obligated to observe the mitzvot, the divine commandments, as they are revealed in the Torah* and the Talmud.† There was no distinction, as there is today, between the religious and the secular. Jews may have been more or less observant, but there were no nonreligious Jews.

Jerry: What about Jews who didn't believe in God or who didn't observe the law?

Rabbi: If they didn't follow the law, the *halacha*, they were considered sinners. They were still Jewish, though.

Jerry: Does the *halacha* say you have to believe in God?

---

*Torah—the first five books of the Bible.
†Talmud—the postbiblical rabbinic elaboration of the Torah.

Rabbi: No, it was assumed that you did. Rather, until modern times, that wasn't really an issue.

Jerry: What caused the split, then, between Jewishness and Judaism?

Rabbi: Two things: first, the Enlightenment and the enormous changes in the conditions of life and thought that followed—changes that undermined the essential assumptions of Judaism; second, Napoleon.

Jerry: Napoleon? What did he have to do with the Jews?

Rabbi: Napoleon affected Jewish life in a profound way. Much of what is now happening in the Jewish world was set in motion by Napoleon.

Jerry: How?

Rabbi: After his military victories were achieved, Napoleon was concerned about the disparate groupings within the new French nation. He wanted to secure their loyalty. He did not want people, such as the Jews, to think of themselves as separate entities with their own laws, their own culture, their own loyalties to anything other than France. He knew very well that the Jews functioned as a "nation" within the larger French nation. He wanted to eliminate such "foreign" nationalities in order to create a single French nation, with all its citizens loyal to the state. So in 1806 he called a meeting of over one hundred Jewish notables of France and presented them with a number of questions designed to clarify what it meant to be Jewish and what the relationship was between the Jews and the state.[1]

The primary question was: Were the Jews a separate nation or a religious community? This was a tough question. If the Jews answered that they were a nation—

meaning, a nation apart from the French nation—they would not be entitled to the rights of citizenship. They would be denying themselves the enormous benefits the new world was offering its citizens. In fact, they *had* functioned pretty much as a separate nation within the larger society. They had their own laws; their own distinctive culture, language, dress, diet. They *looked* different. Napoleon knew this. He needed to get the Jews to commit themselves: Were they Frenchmen loyal to France, or Jews loyal to their own "nation"?

If, on the other hand, they answered that they were a religious community, they would be, in effect, changing the meaning of Judaism: from the all-encompassing way of life it had been previously, to a mere "faith."

Jerry: Some choice.

Rabbi: In answering Napoleon, in effect, *they redefined themselves.* They said, "We are members of the French nation. Our religion is Judaism." That is, they split into two what was previously one: the public and the private. In their public lives, they were to be members of the French nation, citizens loyal to the state. In their private lives, in their homes and in the synagogue, they would be Jews. This is the first time Jews had ever seen themselves in this way. Under Napoleon's pressure, Judaism became an "ism"—a religion, separate from other aspects of life. Henceforth, first in France, then in other countries, including America, the Jews viewed themselves and presented themselves to the world as a religious community, like Catholics and Protestants; but as to their nationality, they were Frenchmen, or Germans, or Americans. The idea that Jewishness is a religious identity was born.

Jerry: What about Jews who didn't see themselves this way— who, for example, didn't believe in God and couldn't fit into a religious definition?

Rabbi: They had a problem. They had either to deny their Jewish-
           ness and leave the Jewish community, as some did, although
           this was not always possible due to the persistence of anti-
           Semitism, which inhibited the freedom of Jews to leave the
           Jewish community. Or, they could pretend that they were
           religious. That is, given the need to define oneself as a Jew
           in religious terms, they could go through the motions of reli-
           gion without being sincerely committed to it.

Jerry: What did most Jews do?

Rabbi: Truly religious Jews—those whom we today would call
           "Orthodox"—chose, in effect, not to enter the new world
           and maintained their commitment to Halachic Judaism.
           Some left Judaism and the Jewish community altogether.
           But a nineteenth-century development "saved" many Jews
           and made it possible for them to be both Jewish and enjoy
           the benefits of the new freedom offered to Jews.

Jerry: Reform Judaism?

Rabbi: Exactly. Reform Judaism and, later, Conservative Judaism
           developed, in part, out of this crisis. Reform Judaism said:
           You can remain Jewish without having to obey the *halacha*.
           The essence of Judaism is not obedience to the laws of the
           Talmud, which are obsolete in this new world, but to the
           moral law, the teachings of the Prophets, the commitment
           to social justice that, said the early reformers, are derived
           from the Bible. What you eat and how you dress and in
           what language you pray are of no importance; what God
           requires of you is that you act righteously. You may, in other
           words, be a patriotic citizen of Germany or America; a
           modern, enlightened citizen of the world; and be a loyal
           Jew all at the same time.

Jerry: So Reform Judaism was a response to Napoleon's challenge?

Rabbi: And to all the other challenges of what we now call moder-
            nity: the Enlightenment, the Emancipation,[2] the Industrial
            Revolution, the rise of science and technology, the spread
            of capitalism—the multiple revolutions and upheavals
            during the past two hundred years that utterly transformed
            the concept of a human being from that of helpless subject
            of mighty forces beyond one's control to that of autono-
            mous, effective, rational being. Reform Judaism explicitly
            stated that the "postulates of reason"[3] are to be of supreme
            importance in determining what is true. Perhaps most
            important of all the ideas of modernity was the concept
            that human beings are created equal, with inalienable indi-
            vidual rights. In response to these new ideas, as well as the
            need to define Jewish identity as a religious identity, Re-
            form created a new way to be Jewish. It spoke realistically
            and positively to emancipated Jews: You don't have to give
            up your identity as Jews in order to enter the world of
            opportunity and freedom. You can be Jewish *and* a modern,
            enlightened human being.

Jerry: But this required a distortion of what it had always meant
            to be a Jew.

Rabbi: Well, it changed the definition dramatically. It reduced
            being Jewish from involvement in an all-encompassing way
            of life governed by divinely authoritative law, to what we
            today know as a religion, an "ism." But it was an ingenious
            solution to an otherwise insoluble problem. For the first
            time in their history, Jews were offered the freedom to be
            whatever they wished—no longer confined to ghettos, no
            longer dependent upon the permission of others. Reform
            Judaism made it possible for enlightened, educated Jews to
            remain Jewish without having to maintain the dietary laws,
            spend hour after hour in shul praying in a language few of
            them understood, and doing and believing all the things
            that were no longer possible for them to do and believe.

Jerry: All they had to give up was their Judaism!

Rabbi: Realize that what you say they were giving up—their pre-
            vious commitment to the *halacha* and the way of life, the
            culture, the religion of the Talmud—was really designed for
            a people in exile, a subjugated people who needed that way
            of life, that culture, that religion for the fifteen centuries
            that followed the destruction of the Second Temple and
            the dispersion of the Jewish people throughout the world.
            That long period was finally over. Had it not been for
            Napoleon and the new concepts of Judaism as a religion
            and Jewishness as a religious identity that he elicited, all
            but a very few Halachic Jews might have abandoned their
            Jewishness altogether.

Jerry: You're saying Reform Judaism saved them from leaving the
            community?

Rabbi: Undoubtedly. But notice the new feature that has now
            entered the picture. In order to be Jewish and to be viewed
            as such by others, it was now necessary to demonstrate one's
            religiousness. It became very important to go to services, to
            pray, to do the things that are considered *religious* behavior.
            Whether or not one believed sincerely in doing these things, that
            is how one demonstrated one's Jewishness.

Jerry: Aha! This explains why today so many Jews go through the
            motions without really believing in God.

Rabbi: Yes, if you want to be Jewish and you think that what
            makes you Jewish is your religion, then you will do "reli-
            gious" things whether or not you are sincerely religious.

Jerry: You're saying that Jews are dishonest about their Judaism?

Rabbi: They don't mean to be. They simply see no alternative. What
            other way do Jews have to demonstrate that they are Jews?

Jerry: They could practice the ethics of Judaism, the morality, the
             values. Isn't this what Reform Judaism said Judaism is all
             about?

Rabbi: What are those values?

Jerry: Justice, compassion, education, family closeness . . .

Rabbi: But there is nothing distinctively Jewish about values. This
             was the contradiction inherent within Reform Judaism.
             Values are universals: If they are valid, they are valid for
             everyone.

Jerry: Isn't it true that we Jews discovered them?

Rabbi: Even if we did—and we did not—these values would now
             be the property of humanity. The law of gravity may have
             been discovered by an Italian, but once discovered it
             became a universal truth and it would be absurd to consider
             it an "Italian principle."

Jerry: Are you saying there are no Jewish values?

Rabbi: Values are values. They have no national or ethnic or reli-
             gious identity. Only people have such identities.

Jerry: Then why is it that we hear so much talk about "Jewish
             values"?

Rabbi: For nonreligious Jews, the fiction that there are "Jewish
             values" that they are upholding gives them the illusion that
             they are still maintaining Judaism. In fact, they are starting
             with the values of their Western, liberal, secular culture
             and then "finding" them in traditional texts. This amounts
             to deciding what is true and then looking for evidence that
             God agrees. Whereas values that are actually demanded by
             the Bible are conveniently ignored.

Jerry: I don't understand.

Rabbi: Take homosexuality. Most enlightened, liberal Jews today advocate "gay rights." To be in favor of such political and social liberalism is considered an expression of "Jewish values." In fact, however, the Bible clearly condemns homosexuality.

Women's equality is another example. The inferior status of women in Halachic Judaism is clearly unacceptable to modern, secular Jews.

Jerry: Are you saying that "Jewish values" are just the values that Jews today endorse?

Rabbi: *Some* Jews. Possibly most Jews. The irony is that truly *religious* Jews—Halachic Jews—often advocate contrary values.

Jerry: I heard an Orthodox rabbi speak out against abortion and in favor of prayer in the public schools.

Rabbi: So you see that the phrase "Jewish values" really boils down to the values that a particular Jewish person or group of Jews prefers.

Jerry: We're back to my original question: If we are not religious and there are no values that we *as Jews* must preserve, why do Jews remain Jewish?

Rabbi: First, we must be clear about the fact that one of the primary forces that has kept Jews together has been anti-Semitism. Even after the Emancipation and the freedom and opportunity it offered Jews, it was still not easy to be a Jew, given the persistence of anti-Semitism. Consider the fact that the most virulent example of anti-Semitism in history occurred barely sixty years ago! Even if Judaism was no longer meaningful to them, most Jews would not betray their history and their people by denying their Jewishness, assuming they could. They had a negative reason, so to speak, to remain Jewish: to resist anti-Semitism. Anti-anti-Semitism became, for many Jews, their "religion."

The past forty or fifty years have changed all that. Today, Jews want to remain Jewish for positive reasons. After all, we are no longer a persecuted group. Being Jewish is no longer a liability, as it was as recently as fifty years ago.[4] No longer does anti-Semitism keep Jews from attending the best universities or living in desirable neighborhoods. Jews today do not suffer disabilities due to their being Jewish. If anything, it is "in" to be Jewish. It is to belong to a highly successful, accomplished community. We can, and do, rise to the top of any occupation or profession. So there is no pressure, as there was until half a century ago, to *not* be Jewish.

Jerry: But surely anti-Semitism is not entirely gone. Synagogues are still vandalized, there are incidents of anti-Semitism on college campuses . . .

Rabbi: There still is some anti-Semitism, but it no longer really affects the lives of Jews as it once did. It used to be structured into the economic, social, and political life of America. Today, it survives on the fringes of society— among certain malcontents. Very few Jews experience anti-Semitism as a significant feature of their lives.

Jerry: There may not be pressure to abandon being Jewish. But what *positive* reason is there to be Jewish? We never seem to get to the heart of the matter: Why do Jews remain Jews?

Rabbi: Most Jews today genuinely want to be Jewish—but for purely secular reasons. First of all, they have not made a conscious decision to abandon Judaism, to give it up.

Rather, they have drifted away from it. It simply does not compel their interest, their commitment. But they feel somewhat guilty or sad. They have a sense that they have lost something precious. They have an unclear idea of just what they have lost, but they have a vague feeling of regret about the lack of Judaism in their lives. They feel no strong urge to recover it. Most will not study it, let alone master the texts that being a knowledgeable Jew requires. Aside from rabbis and professional scholars of Judaism, virtually no one any longer is a serious student of Judaism. I think it is safe to say that, for most Jews, it is enough that they are somehow *associated* with it, identified with it. It is this association with their "heritage" that Jews reaffirm when they return on special occasions, such as Rosh Hashanah or Yom Kippur or Passover. These occasional visits remind them of their history, of the "heritage" that they no longer truly understand or wish to master, of the religion that, to be honest, is no more.

Jerry: But many Jews do want to preserve certain traditions of Judaism.

Rabbi: When Jews speak of traditions that are important to them—lighting candles or reciting the *Kaddish*,* for example—it is the connection to their past that they really are interested in preserving, the connection with the long procession of ancestors that precedes them. In reality, however, Jews today stand outside those traditions. They stand outside the frame of reference, the *halacha*, that gave rise to those traditions. They stand outside Judaism.

Jerry: That is why you call them Jews without Judaism?

Rabbi: Yes, they live their daily lives without regard for—or even knowledge of—the fundamental premises of Judaism: the

---

*Kaddish—the Aramaic prayer recited to commemorate the dead.

covenant and the demands of the Torah and the *halacha*. Most Jews are not even aware that such demands exist.

Jerry: What, then, is going on in all our synagogues and temples? Why do people support them?

Rabbi: If you examine the typical congregation's program, you'll see clearly that what is called Judaism today is actually a secularized version of what used to be religion. What is considered Judaism today is not something that Jews know and practice because of their belief in and commitment to God and His commandments. Rather, it is a random collection of "traditions"—rituals, phrases, and melodies that derive from Judaism but are now disconnected from the belief system that generated them. They give one the feeling of being Jewish—and that is their purpose and that of synagogues and temples: to promote and sustain the feeling of Jewishness in people who are no longer religious. Rabbis urge these activities for what is actually a *secular* reason: to insure the survival of the Jewish people. The reason given for what rabbis typically encourage people to do is not that God requires it, but that it will be good for the children, or the family, or the community.

Jerry: Jews want to be Jewish, but not religious.

Rabbi: Yes, but because they have been taught for two hundred years now that to be Jewish *means* to be religious, to belong to a religious community, to have a "faith"—when they lack that faith, they feel guilty. They feel that they are not authentic Jews. They may go to services now and then, but that only increases their guilt, because the prayers remind them of what they don't believe.

Jerry: But they are *not* authentic Jews! As you said, they stand outside Judaism. The little connection they still have is motivated by nostalgia for something they no longer even care to understand. Shouldn't they feel guilty?

Rabbi: No—unless, of course, they are lying to themselves. If Jews pretend to practice Judaism when, in fact, they are indistinguishable from their non-Jewish neighbors in terms of their daily decisions and behavior, yes, they should feel guilty for their hypocrisy. But there is an alternative.

Jerry: What is the alternative?

Rabbi: Honesty. Relief. Gratitude. Recognizing that the dramatic changes that have benefited the Jews so richly—freedom, individual rights, the opportunity to participate fully in the larger secular society, as well as the rise of science and the ascendancy of reason over faith—are the very forces that have undermined the authority and relevance of Judaism. Recognizing that this is not cause for guilt, but for rejoicing. Two burdens have been lifted from our shoulders: that of persecution at the hands of human authority and that of obedience to supernatural authority. We now are free to enjoy fully the dignity that is the right of all human beings, and we now are free to be honest about our Jewishness.

NOTES

1. For the questions and answers, see Calvin Goldscheider and Alan S. Zuckerman, *The Transformation of the Jews* (Chicago: University of Chicago Press, 1984), pp. 38–39.

2. The release of European Jews, following the French Revolution, from their centuries-long isolation in self-contained communities and their integration into the political, economic, and social life of European society. Now, for the first time, they were able to mingle freely with non-Jews and were exposed to new ideas, liberties, and opportunities that contradicted the ancient teachings, prescriptions, and prohibitions of Judaism.

3. See Reform Judaism's "Pittsburgh Platform" of 1885, pt. 6. For the

complete text of the platform, see Michael A. Meyer, *Response to Modernity* (New York: Oxford University Press, 1988), pp. 387–88.

4. "Think of the changes that have occurred in the past twenty-five or thirty years. When I was growing up, when I became a teacher at Harvard Law School, no matter how good a student a Jew was, or how high he ranked in his class, he couldn't get a job in a Wall Street law firm. I was turned down by thirty-three out of thirty-three Wall Street firms; only one even gave me an interview." Alan M. Dershowitz, "The Not-So-Vanishing American Jew," *Humanistic Judaism* (spring 1998): 31.

CONVERSATION THREE

Who Created Whom?

Mr. G.:   Rabbi, we would like to join your congregation, but I heard you don't believe in God.

Rabbi: Do *you*?

Mr. G.:   How else can you explain the universe?

Rabbi: *Explain* the universe?

Mr. G.:   How it came to be; who created it.

Rabbi: How do you know it was created?

Mr. G.:   Come now, Rabbi. You know what I mean.

Rabbi: I'm serious. How could the universe have been "created"? Out of what? If there was "something" in existence before the universe was created, out of which it was created, what was that "something"? Whatever it was, if it existed, what created it? And out of what? Do you see that to say, "The universe was created," leads to infinite regress? And if you say, "The universe was created out of nothing," what exactly does that mean? How can *nothing* exist? Only *something* can

49

exist. It's impossible for there to have been "something" before the universe existed; and it's impossible for there to have been "nothing" before the universe existed. So, to say "The universe was created" is meaningless.

Mr. G.:   Are you saying the universe has *always* existed?

Rabbi: Exactly. The universe is eternal. It always has existed, and it always will exist. Why is the idea of an eternal universe more difficult to accept than the idea of an eternal God?

Mr. G.:   Okay, so you don't need God in order to have the universe. What about morality? Where do the Ten Commandments come from if not from God?

Rabbi: They come from human experience. Human beings have learned that following certain rules enables us to live together. Ancient people called these rules divine commandments. They were not yet bold enough to take credit for discovering them.

Mr. G.:   But what makes "Thou shalt not kill" true if it's merely a human law?

Rabbi: What makes the law of gravity true?

Mr. G.:   That's different. It's a law of nature. If there were no humans, there would still be a law of gravity.

Rabbi: Correct. Human beings simply discovered the principles operating in the universe. They would exist even if humans didn't.

Mr. G.:   But "Thou shalt not kill" is not like the law of gravity.

Rabbi: True. Without humans, moral principles would be meaningless.

Mr. G.:   They wouldn't exist?

Rabbi: How could they? Moral principles—what used to be called commandments—are rules that human beings have developed, over the centuries, that make civilization and society possible.

Mr. G.:   But they don't come from God?

Rabbi: Suppose they did. Suppose there were a supernatural source for "Thou shalt not kill." Would that make it a good law?

Mr. G.:   It would have to be good if it came from God.

Rabbi: Why? Why couldn't it be a bad law? The Bible contains many laws that we, today, would consider bad, even though God supposedly commanded them.

Mr. G.:   Such as . . .

Rabbi: Such as: If you find a man picking up sticks on the Sabbath, kill him.* Kill the Midianites, including innocent women and children.† Kill a man who lies with another man.‡ Aren't these moral laws that we consider bad? Wouldn't we punish people who obeyed them?

Mr. G.:   But if "Thou shalt not kill" is just a human law, why obey it? What is to stop someone from taking the law into his own hands and killing others just because he feels like it?

Rabbi: Other human beings will stop him.

Mr. G.:   Don't you think we'd have anarchy if people really believe that there is no God to punish them for their sins?

---

*Num. 15:32–36.
†Num. 31:15, 17.
‡Lev. 20:13.

Rabbi: Look at the prison population. Prisons are filled with people who believe in God and believe that they, themselves, are sinners. God and God-based morality haven't prevented the most horrible crimes.

Mr. G.:   But I'm talking about ordinary people, not hardened criminals. Don't you think we need to believe there is a God who is behind "Thou shalt not kill" and who will punish us if we disobey Him?

Rabbi: I think twenty-five centuries of human bloodshed have disproved that thesis. I have a different suggestion: we need to put the responsibility for moral behavior squarely upon human beings, not God. Just as children must outgrow the need for parents to care for them and be responsible for them, so must adult human beings outgrow the need for a Cosmic Parent.

THE FOLLOWING WEEK

Mr. G.:   Rabbi, you really shook me up last time. It's the first time I ever heard of a rabbi not believing in God.

Rabbi: The real question is: How can anyone believe in a being who can think without a brain, who can see without eyes, who is invisible and without any physical attributes, yet lives and has the emotions and all the characteristics of human beings? Does that make sense to you?

Mr. G.:   Well, God is not supposed to make sense.

Rabbi: Why not?

Mr. G.:   Because there are things that just don't make sense, and God explains *them*.

Rabbi: For example?

Mr. G.:   Death.

Rabbi: Death doesn't make sense?

Mr. G.:   Does it to you?

Rabbi: Yes. If animals and trees and insects were to live forever, every inch of space on this planet would long ago have been filled. There would be no room for another living thing.

Mr. G.:   I mean human death. It makes no sense.

Rabbi: Human beings, too, would have run out of room long ago. But more important, if we were to live forever, life would have no meaning, no value. It's only because life is finite that we can appreciate it.

Mr. G.:   Why couldn't we appreciate life that goes on forever?

Rabbi: Because there would *always* be another opportunity to do what we did not do yet. There would be no point in doing anything, if you *knew* that you could do it later—tomorrow, next year, in a thousand years. Death is what makes life important.

Mr. G.:   So you're saying God doesn't "give life and take it away"?

Rabbi: What would that idea mean, if it were true? That God is responsible for the horrible deaths that we, unfortunately, hear about every day—innocent children dying of painful diseases, whole populations starving to death?

Mr. G.:   So there is no point in praying to God for recovery from illness?

Rabbi: I see none.

Mr. G.:   What about the other mysteries that people say that God explains?

Rabbi: Such as?

Mr. G.:   Well, the order in the universe, for example.

Rabbi: Why the Sun is just far enough away from Earth so that we're not fried to a crisp, but far enough away to give us warmth and light?

Mr. G.:   Yes. And that's just one example of the incredible complexity and order in the universe. Take the human eye. More intricate and perfectly designed than any camera. The brain is more powerful than the most sophisticated computer.

Rabbi: You are describing the way things are. The way they have become after eons of development and evolution. Things are this way because it is the only way they can be, given their nature and history. If Earth were closer to the Sun, there would be no Earth. The universe would be different.

Mr. G.:   And we wouldn't be here. Do you see my point?

Rabbi: Perhaps, in that different universe, some far more wonderful creature on some far more beautiful planet would be saying: "How is it that everything is just right for us to exist? If the Sun were just a little closer. . . . There *must* be a God to have created this orderly and incredibly complex universe!"

Mr. G.:   In other words, what we call order is just the way things have to be if there is to be a universe.

Rabbi: *This* universe, yes.

Mr. G.:   But how can you explain the fact that so many people believe in God? How could they all be wrong?

Rabbi: People believed Earth was flat until experience and science proved them wrong. The idea of God made sense to people for many centuries. Today it doesn't. That isn't to say that nobody believes in God. Some people still insist Earth is flat, despite empirical evidence to the contrary. But even among those who say they believe in God, most people don't act on that belief.

Mr. G.:   I don't understand.

Rabbi: Even most "religious" people, when they have a medical problem, call upon doctors and the science of medicine rather than rely upon prayer, as they might have done, say, five hundred years ago.

Mr. G.:   But there was no science of medicine five hundred years ago.

Rabbi: Precisely. At that time, it made sense to pray for relief from illness, given the widespread belief in nonhuman powers that caused illness and provided cures.

Mr. G.:   What about the idea that we pray so that God will give the surgeon the skill to do the operation successfully?

Rabbi: Suppose the surgeon tells you he doesn't believe in God? Would you go looking for one who does?

Mr. G.:   I might.

Rabbi: Suppose you find one, but he has never performed this particular procedure. He tells you that he'll do his best and, "with God's help," you'll live. Which surgeon would you select: this one, or the one who has successfully performed this operation a thousand times but who refuses to pray with you?

Mr. G.: Why not pick the atheist surgeon *and* pray that he will pull me through?

Rabbi: Fine, if that makes you feel better. But your prayer will have no effect upon the surgeon's skill.

Mr. G.: Would you pray for me if I asked you to?

Rabbi: No. I would wish you well. I would support you and en- courage you and be there for you. That's what friends can do. And it is very important for a sick or dying person to have such friends. But it does no one any good to pretend to believe in magic when what one really needs is the best *human* skills available. We are very fortunate that we happen to live at a time and in a place where such skills exceed anything ever available to our ancestors. We ought to be grateful for our good fortune and utilize whatever resources are available to us when we need them, rather than undermine confidence in their source by praying.

Mr. G.: What is the source?

Rabbi: Human ingenuity. Human skills. Human knowledge. Human wisdom. Human experience. Human reason.

Mr. G.: You sound like a college professor. Why do you call yourself a rabbi if you don't believe in God—if what you really believe in is human reason?

Rabbi: Rabbis are teachers. They study Jewish experience and try to convey the meaning of that experience to Jews today.

Mr. G.:   And there are no restrictions on what we may believe?

Rabbi: One of the great benefits of Jewish experience, and of being Jewish, is that we *are* free from belief restrictions. The essence of being Jewish is the freedom to believe whatever truth your mind reveals to you.

Mr. G.:   Even that there is no God?

Rabbi: Especially that. As I understand Jewish experience, it is impossible to believe that an omnipotent and benevolent God has been in charge of our destiny. Where was He during the Crusades? Where was He during the Inquisition? Where was He during the Holocaust?

Mr. G.:   I agree those are difficult questions, but aren't we supposed to have faith that God is doing His job even though we don't always understand how it could be? Isn't that the point of the story of Job?*

Rabbi: That may be the point of the story of Job, but it flies in the face of the past two thousand years of Jewish history. If that history demonstrates anything, it is that we Jews cannot depend upon God to save us. We must save ourselves.

---

*The biblical Book of Job is the story of a thoroughly righteous man whose faith in God is tested when everything he has is taken away from him—his possessions, his home, even his children. Afflicted with a terrible disease and reduced to misery, Job, realizing that he is guilty of no wrong-doing, demands that God justify his suffering. God's answer is that no mere human being can hope to understand the workings of the almighty deity who, after all, created the universe. Job acknowledges that he cannot understand the reasons for evil and suffering and must trust in God's wisdom and ultimate justice. (Job 40:3–5, 42:1–6)

CONVERSATION FOUR

Spirituality

Mr. G.: I hope you don't mind my bringing my wife with me this time.

Rabbi: Not at all.

Mr. G.: When I told her about our conversation last week, and that you confirmed what we had heard about you—that you don't believe in God—she hit me with a hundred questions I can't answer.

Rabbi: Such as?

Mrs. G.: Number one? How can you be a rabbi if you don't believe in God?

Rabbi: Your husband asked me this question, too. "Rabbi" originally meant "master," or, as we would say today, "teacher." The title describes my function, not my beliefs. It's like "professor."

Mrs. G.: Isn't it your function to teach people that they *should* believe in God? But if *you* don't . . .

Rabbi: No, a rabbi as teacher helps people discover what *they* believe, or opens their minds to possibilities that may enlarge their vision.

Mrs. G.:   How does not believing in God enlarge my vision?

Rabbi: By clarifying the fact that you, and only you, are in charge of your life. There is no supernatural, transcendent being to whom you may turn for help. Each of us must broaden our sense of responsibility for our decisions, our behavior, our lives. This enlargement of human responsibility simultaneously frees us from many restrictions that inhibit people who depend upon a nonhuman authority for answers and guidance.

Mrs. G.:   Aren't you overlooking the *spiritual* part of our lives?

Rabbi: What do you mean by "spiritual"?

Mrs. G.:   I mean what we can't see with our eyes yet know is there.

Rabbi: Are you saying that our five senses are insufficient to experience reality?

Mrs. G.:   Not only that. I'm saying there is much, much more to reality than what our minds can grasp. There is a reality beyond this world, something higher, something that gives this world purpose and meaning.

Rabbi: How do you know this spiritual dimension is real? Do you have access to it?

Mrs. G.:   Sometimes when I watch a beautiful sunset or while walking in my garden or when I see my daughter's smile . . . I feel a sense of inner peace and even a connection to the universe that I can't explain but is as real as the things I can touch and see.

| Rabbi: | Do you have these experiences without using your five senses? |

Mrs. G.:   It's when I *close* my eyes and *turn off* my senses and go deep within myself . . . that's when I feel spiritual.

Rabbi: You are suggesting that there are two realities: material and spiritual.

Mrs. G.:   Exactly. And we need both. But without the spiritual, the material is meaningless. It's the petty world of getting and spending. It's the world of trivial pursuits and selfish passions. It's the world of problems and pain and illness and death. With all due respect, Rabbi, you are too much into your head. There is more to life than thinking. We have hearts. We feel as well as think.

Rabbi: Don't misunderstand me. I, too, experience moments of great emotional satisfaction. I appreciate the beauty of a great painting or symphony. I feel a wonderful serenity when I gaze at the ocean. When I play with my granddaughter, I am overcome with joy. These experiences are indeed what make life rich and exciting and meaningful.

Mrs. G.:   You *are* a spiritual person.

Rabbi: Let's say there are two kinds of spirituality: mystical and natural. Mystical spirituality presumes that there is a non-human power or intelligence or being "out there"—and it need not be called God—with whom human beings can communicate or connect. When they do, they are in touch with the source of meaning, of value, of life itself. To be connected with this "higher power" is to feel at one with the universe, with nature, and in harmony with all there is. A "spiritual person" is one who is unconcerned with this physical world and its immediate, mundane concerns, and is focused instead upon that which is truly significant and eternal.

Mrs. G.:   I take it that this is not your brand of spirituality.

Rabbi: Correct. My brand, as you put it, is natural spirituality, which acknowledges that we are more than our material selves. We are more than highly developed computers. We cannot be reduced to bundles of synapses and electrical charges. We have hopes and dreams. We feel and worry. We make decisions. We make mistakes. We are unpredictable. This is what it means to be human. We are free to think and feel, achieve and fail, love and hate. It is this freedom that is essential to our humanity. There is, according to the current state of our knowledge, no other living thing that possesses such freedom. This freedom makes each human being unique. Until now, science has not identified in material terms what the self is—what makes me different from you. One day, perhaps, the self, or soul, or essence of a person will be understood completely; although I doubt that we will ever reach complete knowledge of what makes us tick—and, until we do, we may rationally believe that there is something called "the human spirit" that is quite real, yet beyond scientific analysis.

Mrs. G.:   I don't understand the difference between mystical and natural spirituality. Isn't "your" brand also mystical?

Rabbi: The difference is that natural spirituality locates everything that we think and feel within us, within our natural bodies. To be specific, within our brains, or, I prefer to say, within our minds, because "brain" suggests raw matter and I mean that we are more than mere material. By "mind" I mean the brain and all of the results of its use—including the choices and decisions we have made over a lifetime, the values we have developed, the experiences we have enjoyed and suffered, and how we have interpreted those experiences. What I do not mean is that there is some kind of disembodied spirit outside ourselves with whom we connect.

Mrs. G.:   Isn't love a connection? Isn't the feeling you have with your granddaughter a connection?

Rabbi: Of course. We—that is, our minds—connect with one another. That is what you and I are doing right now. We are using our minds to communicate with one another. Whether one is an artist or writer or rabbi, reaching another human being's understanding by means of one's reason and emotions is what I mean by our spiritual connection. It is a horizontal connection, though, not vertical. Meaning, instead of relating to a "higher power" up there, above and beyond humanity, we relate to other human beings.

Mrs. G.:   How do you know there is no spirit "out there"?

Rabbi: There simply is no evidence for such a presence. If we can explain our experience without referring to a nonhuman consciousness, why assume one exists?

Mrs. G.:   Why do so many intelligent people believe in "disembodied spirits," as you call them? Are you saying they're all mistaken?

Rabbi: Most people, however intelligent, do not give careful, sustained thought to the questions we are discussing. It is still respectable in our time and place to believe in God and in the existence of "spiritual" entities, and many people simply accept such beliefs without question. It may even appear arrogant to them to insist that there is no God.

Mr. G.:   That's exactly what my wife said to me when I told her about our conversation: "It's arrogant to assert that there is no God."

Mrs. G.:   That is what I said, Rabbi. Can you prove there isn't one?

Rabbi: It's impossible to prove that something does not exist. Can you prove that invisible pink elephants are not floating about in this room? The burden of proof always rests with the one who makes a positive claim—such as, that God—or any form of disembodied spirit—exists. I am quite willing to examine any evidence that would support such a claim. Absent the evidence, I'm skeptical. Just as I am about witches, goblins, and Santa Claus.

Mrs. G.:   You're more than skeptical, you're an atheist!

Rabbi: Yes, I am. Atheist means "without theism." I am lacking the belief in a being for which there is no evidence.

Mr. G.:   That's good enough for me.

Mrs. G.:   But not for me. You said you experience beauty. Do you really think flowers and mountains and rainbows just happen to be beautiful? That there is no divine spirit that created such beauty?

Rabbi: Beauty is entirely a human invention. Beauty *is* in the eye of the beholder.

Mrs. G.:   That may be true of music and art. Who is to say that this painting is more beautiful than that? But what about the beauty in nature? You as much as said there is such beauty.

Rabbi: There is no beauty in nature. We humans impose such value judgments as "beauty" upon nature.

Mrs. G.:   A sunrise is not beautiful? My garden is not beautiful?

Rabbi: You think so, and I think so, but objectively there is no such thing as beauty. We perceive—by means of our senses—colors and shapes that we decide constitute beauty. But in reality, a rainbow is no more beautiful than a weed. Nature just is—it is neither beautiful nor ugly.

Mrs. G.: Why is my feeling of beauty so powerful if it's all just in *me*?

Rabbi: Precisely because it comes from within you. The power of love, of fear, and of all the emotions, as well as beauty, is due entirely to our perceptions, our values, our experiences. The mistake made by mystics and theists is in attributing the source of our emotions and values to something outside of us.

Mrs. G.: When I have the feeling of serenity, say, when I'm gardening or listening to Mozart—it's coming from me?

Rabbi: Exactly. Neither nature nor Mozart gives us serenity. Nor does God. It is a product of the "human spirit" in *you*, which is a powerful thing, indeed!

Mrs. G.: It's difficult for me to believe that all of these feelings are coming from me. I've always thought that I'm just a receiver of nature's beauty, or of God's love, or of the gift of *some* spiritual power in the universe that is the source of beauty and meaning. Doesn't your "natural spirituality" diminish the importance of the values you mentioned—if they're just human values?

Rabbi: On the contrary. I appreciate beauty and love all the more because I am aware that I and other human beings are entirely responsible for creating and promoting these values, as well as the conditions that make them possible. I am all the more motivated to fight against injustice because I know that it, too, is a human creation and requires human power if it is to be eliminated.

Mrs. G.: So, we are alone in the universe?

Rabbi: Just as bugs and bacteria are "alone" in the universe, so are we. Again, this understanding enhances the meaning of human friendship—that is, of our spiritual connection. It is not a mystical gift from above. It requires our initiative, our commitment, our sensitivity, and many other human qualities. It is our gift to one another, as are peace, happiness, and all the values we cherish that make life rich and fulfilling.

Mr. G.:   I like the rabbi's brand of spirituality. It doesn't require me to pray or remove myself from the world. It gives me a sense of purpose without the rigmarole of religion.

Mrs. G.:   Maybe you're right.

A WEEK LATER

Rabbi: I hope our discussion last week didn't disturb you, Mrs. G.

Mrs. G.:   Actually, it inspired me. I realize that I'm a spiritual person in more respects than I ever thought. I have spiritual potential that I haven't yet fulfilled.

Rabbi: Good! But you said on the phone that you have another question.

Mrs. G.:   Just one. If all of our values come from within us, and if what I think is beautiful is the result of my own values and experience, aren't all judgments just a matter of personal taste? Who is to say that Gandhi was a better person than Hitler? Or that Mozart is better music than some piece of hard rock that *I* think is just noise?

Rabbi: My answer is that whatever utilizes or exhibits the most distinctively *human* qualities and abilities is "better" than what does not. Mozart is better music because it is more demanding—intellectually, emotionally, and, yes, spiritually—than is elevator music. It is also more rewarding. It calls upon the performer and listener to cultivate the highest human attributes in order to express, understand, and appreciate the music.

Mrs. G.:   Highest?

Rabbi: I knew you would question that word. By "highest," I mean, again, the most uniquely *human* and *spiritual* attributes, as distinguished from those merely physical abilities that we share with other animals. I have in mind such abilities as thinking, feeling, remembering, dreaming, hoping, judging. Animals—so far as we know—lack these abilities. They may feel pain and pleasure and act so as to avoid the one and seek the other, but they are unable to reflect on their behavior. They do not decide to postpone immediate gratification for the sake of more significant long-term goals. They lack the ability to conceptualize, to formulate opinions and judgments, to distinguish between right and wrong. Animals behave on the basis of instinct. We act on the basis of choice. We are the only living things capable of morality.

Mrs. G.:   Why not say human attributes are just different from other animals'? Why do you insist that they are higher?

Rabbi: Because they enable us to improve the quality of our lives. They are the basis of civilization—of agriculture and art and medicine and of all the creations of which only humans are capable. Raw physical power is not our most distinctive characteristic. Other animals are superior to us in strength, speed, and agility. We cannot fly. But our use of reason has enabled us to reach the moon.

Mrs. G.:   Why is reaching the moon, or building a skyscraper, or writing a symphony "better" than building a nest?

Rabbi: "Better" insofar as it is more suitable to human needs.

Mrs. G.:   Are you saying that we human beings and our needs are the standard of what is good?

Rabbi: Yes, we are the only living things for whom "good" is meaningful. Other living things either survive or do not. We not only are capable of survival (that is, if we utilize our most distinctively human abilities) but can constantly make our lives more satisfying and less difficult.

Mrs. G.:   Who is to say what is more satisfying? Who decides what improves the quality of our lives?

Rabbi: Each of us decides for himself or herself.

Mrs. G.:   We're back to Gandhi and Hitler. Suppose I decide that killing Jews improves the lives of the rest of the nation— does that give me the right to murder other human beings?

Rabbi: Of course not. No one has the right to impose her values upon others. Because natural spirituality, lacking belief in an external authority such as a God who issues commands and determines correct values, requires respect for the human spirit in each person—even when we disagree. Without an objectively verifiable source of truth outside ourselves, we have no alternative but to "live and let live." Pursue your own happiness and allow others to pursue theirs.

Mrs. G.:   You sound so idealistic.

Rabbi: I hope so.

CONVERSATION FIVE

Anti-Anti-Semitism

Mrs. B.:   Rabbi, I have to talk to you about my son.

Rabbi: Jeff?

Mrs. B.:   Yes. Jeff has had a terrible anti-Semitic experience, and I don't know what to do.

Rabbi: Tell me about it.

Mrs. B.:   The other day he got a call from his girlfriend, Katie. She was in tears. They were supposed to spend spring break in Florida at her grandparents' condo. She said everything was all set, but she called her grandfather just to remind him of their plans and he asked what her boyfriend's name is. She said: "Jeff Cohen," and there was a long silence. She said, "Grandpa, are you all right?" Finally, he answered: "Katie, I'm very sorry but we can't have you two come here next week." "What?" she said, "What's wrong?" There was another long pause, and her grandfather said—and I'm using his exact words: "Jews are not welcome in our home."

Rabbi: He didn't know Jeff is Jewish?

Mrs. B.:   No, it had never come up. I guess Katie had never men-
            tioned his last name.

Rabbi: What happened next?

Mrs. B.:   Katie was devastated. She told her parents. They said there
            was nothing they could do. They love Jeff. He is over at
            their house more than at ours. And her parents told him
            they don't want this to change anything. But they told
            Katie that her grandfather has always had "this thing"
            about Jews. Nobody else in the family agrees with him, but
            they've given up talking to him about it.

Rabbi: How does Jeff feel about it?

Mrs. B.:   He couldn't care less. He says he doesn't love Katie's grand-
            father; he loves her. And he thinks her parents are great.
            The problem is my husband. When he heard about it, he
            was furious. He told Jeff he doesn't want him to see Katie if
            that's the way her family feels about Jews. My husband is
            very upset.

Rabbi: And you?

Mrs. B.:   I'm right in the middle, as usual. I don't see why Katie's
            grandfather's prejudice should affect Katie and Jeff. Her
            parents are lovely people. Katie is the best thing that has
            ever happened to Jeff. They are practically engaged! But my
            husband thinks I should back him up. He wants *me* to talk
            to Jeff and Katie and explain why they can't see each other
            anymore.

Rabbi: Can you do it?

Mrs. B.:   No. That's why I'm here. I don't know what to do.

Rabbi: I'd be happy to talk to your husband, if you think it would help.

Mrs. B.:   I was hoping you'd say that. I want to warn you, though. When it comes to anti-Semitism, you don't fool around with my husband. His family was wiped out by the Nazis.

THREE DAYS LATER

Mr. B.:   Thank you for seeing me, Rabbi. My wife told me that you know about our problem.

Rabbi: She told me you were upset about Katie's grandfather.

Mr. B.:   Upset? That miserable so-and-so. I could kill him with my bare hands!

Rabbi: Are you angry with Katie, too?

Mr. B.:   No, I'm not angry with her. She's a doll. But I can't allow my son to marry the granddaughter of an anti-Semite. I can't have grandchildren whose great-grandfather hates Jews. He and his kind wiped out my family. If it were up to him, you and I wouldn't be here.

Rabbi: You feel very strongly about people who dislike Jews.

Mr. B.:   Rabbi, they murdered my family! If it were up to Katie's grandfather, you and I would be in the ovens. Who was it who said we can't give Hitler a posthumous victory? There is no way I can accept Katie in my family.

Rabbi: Is it fair to punish Katie for the sin of her grandfather?

Mr. B.:   Fair? Was it fair to destroy six million innocent people— babies, women, old people who could barely walk? No, I'm not interested in being fair. I say, "Never again!" Never again will the Jews be victims.

Rabbi: I agree. And we can't let anti-Semites control our lives.

Mr. B.:   You said it. I spend most of my free time fighting anti-Semitism. I work for six different organizations. I give more money to fight anti-Semitism than I spend on my own health. I have nothing against Katie, personally. She's a beautiful, lovely girl. But not for my son.

Rabbi: I respect your feelings, Mr. B. But I have to tell you, I'm uncomfortable when I hear you say, "I have nothing against so-and-so, personally." Doesn't it sound very much like those who say, "I have nothing against that Jew or that black, personally, but not in my neighborhood"?

Mr. B.:   This is different. We're talking about ovens. We're talking about the systematic slaughter of an entire people.

Rabbi: I understand. But Hitler was defeated and the system he created was destroyed. Thanks to the Nazis, anti-Semitism is clearly acknowledged as the foul, barbaric, and very dangerous prejudice that you and I—and many good Christians, too—despise. Isn't it counterproductive to create or imagine anti-Semitism where it doesn't exist?

Mr. B.:   It *does* exist. Katie's grandfather could be living next door!

Rabbi: But Katie, herself—why label her with her grandfather's prejudice? Isn't that a prejudice itself? Prejudging a person because of another person's faults? Katie loves your son. Her parents love him. They have explicitly disassociated themselves from the grandfather's anti-Semitism. How can we ever go beyond the past and its awful prejudices, if we, ourselves, don't abandon our prejudices?

Mr. B.:   Rabbi, call me prejudiced. But I am loyal to my family. To my people. To my relatives who were killed because they were Jews. There is no way I will defile their memory by accepting that girl in my family.

ONE WEEK LATER

Jeff: Rabbi, I can't thank you enough for talking to my father. He told me you think he should forget about Katie's grandfather.

Rabbi: Not exactly. I told him I didn't think it was fair to reject Katie because of her grandfather's prejudice.

Jeff: That's what I keep telling him. I've never even met the guy. And I don't want to. Katie has said she won't even visit him herself. She hasn't got an ounce of anti-Semitism in her. Why can't I get my father to see that?

Rabbi: Your father has been deeply wounded by the tragic experience of his family. He sees himself as the guardian of their memory and believes it's his sacred duty to fight against anti-Semitism in every way possible. Actually, he isn't that different from many Jews who, for understandable reasons, have made anti-anti-Semitism their religion.

Jeff: Their religion?

Rabbi: The Holocaust has so deeply affected them that, to them, being Jewish *means* fighting against anti-Semitism. To a greater or lesser degree, this is true of Jews in general. They have very little, if any, real attachment to Judaism. They still feel Jewish. Some feel deeply Jewish. But in a secular sense. In an ethnic sense. And this translates into being sensitive to every conceivable manifestation of anti-Semitism.

Jeff: That's my father. He never goes to services. He thinks prayer is nonsense. On Passover, as far as he's concerned, if all we do is have a special dinner with matzos and wine, it's a seder. But every year, he always, *always* brings up the Holocaust. He says it's what Passover is really about. Making sure it never happens again.

Rabbi: So you see that this problem with Katie's grandfather reaches deeply into your father's whole sense of his Jewishness: Being Jewish is to fight against anti-Semitism. Katie's grandfather is an anti-Semite. Therefore, everything associated with that man must be rejected. He can't allow himself to be rational about it.

Jeff: I respect my father's feelings. But he's wrong. And I'm not going to let him destroy my relationship with Katie. I'm going to continue seeing her, and I'll probably marry her. He's going to have to change his mind, or . . .

Rabbi: Let me know if there is anything I can do.

Jeff: Thank you.

TWO MONTHS LATER

Jeff: Rabbi, Katie and I would like you to officiate at our wedding.

Rabbi: Mazal tov! When will it take place?

Jeff: Soon. We haven't worked out all the details yet.

Rabbi: How is your father taking it?

Jeff: He says he won't come to the wedding. My mother says when the time comes, he'll probably change his mind. But I don't think so.

Rabbi: What about Katie's grandfather? Will he attend?

Katie: Absolutely not! I've made it clear that he is not welcome. Not that he'd come, anyway.

Rabbi: So you've talked to him about his remark?

Katie: I went down to visit him. I told him I was furious with him but felt I owed it to him to talk it out with him. He said there was nothing to talk about. He thinks Jews are Christ-killers and all the rest—I couldn't believe what I was hearing! I asked him why I never had heard this from him before. He said there was no reason to bring it up. Not until he found out my boyfriend was Jewish. I said I was ashamed of him. I told him I planned to marry Jeff, and he said if I did I would be violating centuries of "family tradition." I said, "Good. It's about time somebody did." He told me to get out of his house and not come back.

Rabbi: That must have been very upsetting.

Katie: It was, but after a while I began to realize that I was glad this had happened. If it hadn't, I wouldn't have known something about my grandfather that it's important to know. And I have tremendous respect for my parents. It's tough on them, on my mother especially, but I'm really proud of her. She told me that she had always hoped I would be married before my grandfather died so that he could have the pleasure of knowing his great-grandchildren, but that my happiness is more important and she knows that Jeff is right for me.

Jeff: This has brought Katie and me closer, too. I realize more than ever how much she loves me. And I think her parents have been just great. I wish I could say the same for my father.

Rabbi: Maybe your mother is right. Perhaps your father will come around, once he sees that you're going to be married despite his objections.

Jeff: Possibly. What really bothers him is not knowing his grand-children. But he told me he would rather not ever see them than to see in their faces the image of the murderers of his family. That really hurt. I told him that if this is what being Jewish has come to mean, I don't want any part of it.

Rabbi: You realize, though, that this is not true. Your father does not speak for anybody but himself.

Jeff: Yes, but as you said, and as I have observed myself since you pointed it out, this religion of anti-anti-Semitism can go to ridiculous extremes: seeing anti-Semitism under every rock, imagining it where it doesn't exist. It's almost as if some Jews want there to be anti-Semitism so that they have something to fight against, something to remind them that they are Jewish.

CONVERSATION SIX

The Naysayers

Linda: Rabbi, I was reading a list of "The 100 Most Famous Jews of the Twentieth Century" and was surprised to see so many important artists, scientists, and writers—some of whom I hadn't realized were Jewish. How do you explain the fact that so many secular Jews have been so prominent? I'm thinking of such people as Sigmund Freud, Albert Einstein, Gustav Mahler, Karl Marx, Darius Milhaud, Maurice Ravel, Arnold Schoenberg, Kurt Weill, Gertrude Stein, Ayn Rand, Steven Spielberg, Irving Berlin . . . the list seems endless.

Rabbi: And you correctly point out that they are secular, not religious, Jews. None of the most famous Jews of the past one hundred years has been known for his or her religious devotion or for his or her contribution to religious life. They have been scientists, artists, critics, philosophers, entrepreneurs.

Linda: People who, it seems to me, have been on the cutting edge of the culture.

Rabbi: Yes, people willing and able to challenge prevailing opinion and the authorities of the day.

Linda: Is it an accident that they were Jews?

Rabbi: I don't think it was an accident. Consider the most basic fact about the Jews over the past two thousand years. What do they all have in common?

Linda: I hope you're not referring to their faith in God.

Rabbi: No, who knows how many had this faith?

Linda: Or to any other religious belief.

Rabbi: I'm thinking of something they *didn't* believe and which is the one thing that set them apart from others in their world.

Linda: They refused to accept other religions?

Rabbi: More specifically, they said "no" to Christianity. Christianity addressed Jews directly, as it addressed no other community, because Jesus, himself, was a Jew, as were his disciples and all the founders of Christianity. Why, Christians have asked, did the people of Jesus not accept him as their Lord?

Linda: If they had, they would not be Jews.

Rabbi: Right. Once Christianity had established itself as a religion in its own right, distinct from the Judaism out of which it emerged, Jews were those who said "no" to Christ as savior.

Linda: There were many others who said "no" to Christ: pagans, Moslems . . .

Rabbi: Other non-Christians do not *necessarily* say "no" to Christ. Jews do. The Jews were the *people* of Christ and, as such, were the only people directly addressed by Christianity, *challenged* by Christianity, to accept Christ. Jewish sacred writings were also those of Christianity. The essential difference between the two religions was the belief in Christ.

Linda: Just remaining a Jew, then, was itself a denial of Christianity.

Rabbi: Not only that. When a Jew said "no" to Christianity, everyone close to him—his family, friends, teachers—everyone he loved and respected—assured him he was doing the *right* thing. Those who mattered to him most told him, in effect, that he was being *virtuous* in denying the truth that the rest of the world took for granted.

Linda: Then just being *Jewish* was virtuous, insofar as it implied saying "no" to Christianity.

Rabbi: This is a very important fact about being Jewish. Jews could not help but think of their Jewishness as being good, which, of course, reinforced their commitment to remaining Jewish.

Linda: I see how saying "no" to Christianity strengthened the resolve of religious Jews. But what does it have to do with Jews today, with secular Jews—with Freud, for example?

Rabbi: We must not overlook the fact that the concept of Christ was perhaps the most important single idea of Western civilization. It dominated not merely Christianity but Western culture for almost two thousand years. Consider the extent to which Christian themes and symbols pervade the art, literature, music, and philosophy of Western culture. In saying "no" to Christianity, Jews were simultaneously saying "no" to a large part of Western culture. And, again, they felt virtuous in doing so.

Linda: So they rejected more than just the idea of Christ.

Rabbi: To be Jewish was to be an outsider. It was to be separate
              from the majority in every sense: physically, psychologi-
              cally, culturally, religiously. Do you see what a profound
              impact this had on the attitude of Jews? To be Jewish meant
              that it was *good* to not be part of the majority. To be Jewish
              meant that it was *good* to question the prevailing wisdom of
              the world. To be Jewish meant that it was *good* to challenge
              not just what others believed about God, but others' beliefs
              about everything—and to be supported in this nay-saying
              by one's parents, one's ancestors, one's community.

Linda: I'm uncomfortable that being Jewish is essentially a nega-
              tive identity.

Rabbi: Actually, it is quite positive. In saying "no" to the central
              myth of Western culture, Jews are released from precom-
              mitments of any kind. This is a very *positive* position. It
              made possible unprecedented achievements in many fields
              of endeavor. Our history as rejectors of the single idea that
              unites all Christians grants us the freedom to question *all*
              beliefs, *all* ideas, *all* assumptions. No, it isn't an accident
              that so many of the most daring minds of the past two cen-
              turies were Jews. Freud is a particularly interesting example,
              for he challenged not only the prevailing psychological
              wisdom of the day and thereby created a new way of seeing
              humanity, but he also challenged the idea of religion itself,
              concluding that it is an illusion.

Linda: Are you suggesting that his *Jewishness* caused him to chal-
              lenge religion?

Rabbi: In a sense. It gave him permission to be the bold naysayer
              enabling him to see what others could not see.

Linda:	Was he really Jewish, though? Did he think of himself as a Jew?
Rabbi:	Absolutely. Not only did he not deny his Jewishness, he asserted it. He was proud of it. He even said that it was responsible for his "independence of judgment."[1] And, to this day, he is regarded *by Jews* as one of the greatest Jews in history, despite his atheism.
Linda:	So you're saying our ability to say "no" to Christ enables us to go beyond the prevailing opinion and, in this respect, is a positive ability.
Rabbi:	All great discoveries begin with a "no." You have to question what is assumed or taken for granted. If you can't say "no" to the status quo, you will never proceed beyond it to new understandings.
Linda:	Is this the role of the Jews in the modern world? To be naysayers? Is this our purpose, our reason to be Jews?
Rabbi:	No one can assert what our role or purpose is, as Jews. I suggest that our heritage of nay-saying explains the prominence of Jews in so many creative fields. It also gives each one of us a sense of what being Jewish may mean in the modern world, now that religion is virtually gone from our lives. After all, we still say "no" to Christ. We still are, in this respect, outsiders.[2] We still refuse to participate in the dominant mythology of Western culture, and in doing so, we are free in a sense and to a degree that no other group is free.[3]
Linda:	But non-Jews also make important discoveries, are creative, are free . . .
Rabbi:	Of course. Yet ours is the only history whose central theme is that of rejection and of being rejected. It is our tradition,

so to speak, to reject the common wisdom of the day. It is much easier for Jews, therefore, to be iconoclasts, innovators, path breakers. Others first have to free themselves from their ancestral ideology, from the conventional beliefs of their culture, before they can achieve the freedom that Jews have simply by virtue of being Jewish. Christians or those from a Christian background are not as free as are Jews from the conventional beliefs and values at the center of Western culture.[4] For example, it would be far more difficult, would it not, for a Christian to deny God?

Linda: She would have to deny Christianity.

Rabbi: Of course. One must believe in God in order to be a Christian. But regardless of how radical one's ideas may be, a Jew does *not* have to deny her Jewishness.

Linda: One can be a Jew and not believe in God?

Rabbi: Large numbers of Jews today are atheists.

Linda: Jews can believe *anything*?

Rabbi: Jews are free to pursue truth wherever it may lead, regardless of the consequences. That, I suggest, is the most significant meaning of Jewishness today.

A WEEK LATER

Linda: I've been thinking about the concept that Jews are free to believe anything.

Rabbi: Their Jewishness does not depend upon what they believe.

Linda: But not all Jews are bold truth seekers. There are some very conventional Jews. Some of my best friends . . .

Rabbi: We are not *required* to exercise our freedom to think boldly. Just as all human beings are free to utilize whatever talents and abilities they have, but are not required to do so. The historical experience of the Jews has bestowed upon them a unique degree of freedom. But they are free not to use it.

Linda: Are those who do use it more Jewish? Are Freud and other Jewish atheists better Jews than the rabbis who condemn them?

Rabbi: They are more faithful to their heritage as naysayers, as challengers of the status quo, as trailblazers. I don't like to use such phrases as "better Jews" or "more Jewish."

Linda: It seems strange to think that Jews who don't believe in God are "more faithful to their heritage" than those who do believe in God.

Rabbi: For the past two hundred years we have become so accustomed to the artificial religious definition of the Jews that it is difficult to see ourselves as we really are.

Linda: This concept of nay-saying gives Jews a new sense of the value of being Jewish, doesn't it?

Rabbi: I think this is the most exciting time to be Jewish in our entire history. We do not suffer from persecution. We are no longer bound by the constraints of the *halacha*. We have opportunities undreamed of by our ancestors. We can and do rise to the very top of the culture, in all its aspects—academic, artistic, political, entrepreneurial. For the first time, we are truly free: free to be and do what we wish, free to seek truth wherever our minds and experience lead us, free to express our Jewishness however we wish. And in exercising this freedom, we are most truly Jewish.

NOTES

1. Quoted in Peter Gay, *A Godless Jew* (New Haven: Yale University Press, 1987), p. 136.

2. "Most American adults—about 85 percent in recent surveys, but dropping—identify themselves as Christians." Stephen L. Carter, *The Culture of Disbelief* (New York: Anchor Books, 1993), p. 85. See also p. 86 on America as a "Christian nation."

3. "I've always considered it a privilege to be a Jew. It's a great opportunity to be somewhat marginal—and not entirely voluntarily, either—and to be able to see things not so apparent to people cozily on the inside." Author, historian, and Librarian Emeritus of the Library of Congress Daniel Boorstin, quoted in *Insight* (July 17, 1989): 89.

4. "Because I was a Jew, I found myself free from many prejudices which limited others in the employment of their intellects, and as a Jew I was prepared to go into opposition and to do without the agreement of the 'compact majority.'" Gay, *A Godless Jew*, p. 137, quoting from Freud's letter to members of B'nai B'rith (May 6, 1926).

CONVERSATION SEVEN

A Kids' Roundtable

Jon: In camp last summer, the kids made fun of me because I don't believe in God.

Rabbi: How did they know what you don't believe?

Jon: When we had services, I wouldn't say the prayers. They asked me why and I told them.

Rabbi: Did it bother you that you were different from the others?

Jon: Not that I was different. It bothered me that they made fun of me.

Rabbi: What did they say?

Jon: They said I'm not really Jewish. They called our temple a church.

Rabbi: How did you respond?

Jon: I told them they were crazy.

Sarah: I've had the same kind of experience. When I go to bat mitzvah services at other congregations, I just sit there. I don't really participate. Sometimes, a friend will notice and ask me why I don't say the prayers and I tell her I don't believe in prayer.

Rabbi: Do your friends make fun of you, too?

Sarah: Not exactly. They just think I'm weird. It's like, if you're Jewish you have to say certain things and if you don't, you're strange.

Rabbi: What do your parents say about this?

Jon: Mine keep telling me not to pay any attention to the other kids. But that doesn't really help, because when I'm with them I can't just ignore them.

David: My parents told me I should just say the prayers and not make a problem for myself. When we go to my grandparents' house, we always say the prayers on Friday night or on Passover, and my father says it would offend his parents if we told them that we are humanists* and don't believe in God.

Sarah: We do that, too, when we go to my grandparents' for holidays. My mother told us kids that when you are in someone else's house, you do what they do.

Rabbi: Do you agree?

Sarah: Not really. If they were Christians, should we pretend that we believe in Christ?

---

*Humanists focus upon the importance of human power, wisdom, and achievement rather than the supremacy of a deity.

Rabbi: Good point. It's interesting that many Jews who wouldn't think of reciting prayers addressed to Christ consider it okay to address a god they don't believe in—just to satisfy other Jews.

Ken: What gets me is that some of my friends—and their parents—don't believe in God any more than I do. But they say this is what Jews should do, whether or not they believe.

David: The thing is, most kids—*and* their parents—don't even understand what they mean when they say they believe in God. Whenever I have these discussions with my friends, they say you can't explain the universe without a Creator—but when I point out that you *can*, they switch to some other argument, such as, that without God there would be no morality.

Jon: Right. My aunt is always telling me that if people didn't believe in a Supreme Being who will punish them if they are bad, the world would be a jungle. It makes no difference to her when I remind her of all the murderers who say they believe in God.

Sarah: My favorite argument is that the Jews are God's "Chosen People" and that we have to pray to him or he will be angry and punish us. That's really sick. Where was he during the Holocaust? If he's so powerful and good, how can he permit little babies to suffer and die? It's insulting to be told I have to believe in such a god.

Rabbi: Do you ever think that maybe you should just give in, go along with the crowd, and not be so different?

Sarah: No way! As you told us, Rabbi, if Jewish history teaches anything, it is the importance of standing up for what you believe. Some Jews died for what they believed. Why should I give in, just because some other kid thinks I'm weird?

Jon: It's easy to say we should stand up for what we believe in, but when you're in the situation and kids are ridiculing you and telling you you're not Jewish . . .

Sarah: That's exactly when we have to be strong and not give in.

Ken: It doesn't do any good to argue with people over these things. You just have to be true to yourself and not be worried about what other people think of you.

David: Even when they're your grandparents?

Sarah: If your grandparents love you, they will respect whatever you believe.

David: I know that, but I don't want to hurt their feelings by disagreeing with beliefs that are so important to them. There's no way they'll understand my point of view, so why make them unhappy?

Rabbi: David is concerned not with what others think of him but with their feelings. Do you see a difference between the two problems?

Sarah: Definitely. I can see why you wouldn't want to offend your grandparents. Maybe it's okay to not be so honest if you're trying to protect someone else's feelings. I mean, when someone asks you if you like her new dress, you wouldn't say it's the ugliest dress you've ever seen. It's all right to lie a little in these situations. But when that isn't the issue—when it's what others think of you, then I think you have to be open and honest, and if they don't like it, too bad.

Rabbi: Maybe Sarah has come up with a useful principle to help us handle our unconventional ideas. Our intention is not to make other people—friends *or* grandparents—angry or uncomfortable, but to be true to ourselves. We wouldn't offend members of other religious communities by flaunting our disbelief in Christ or Mohammed—or God. But neither would we want to misrepresent ourselves by offering prayers. Without compromising our convictions, we can attend a theistic service or seder so long as we do not recite words we do not believe. If we are challenged to explain why we are not participating, we may answer honestly. If others are unhappy with us, well, that's *their* problem. On the other hand, we needn't go out of our way to draw attention to our differences, especially if doing so would be offensive.

Jon: That doesn't solve my problem with my camp friends.

David: Or mine with my grandparents.

Rabbi: Not all problems can be solved. We can go only so far in respecting others' points of view, and then it's up to them to do the same.

Jon: It's not easy to be a humanistic Jew.

Ken: That's one of the reasons I like it!

A WEEK LATER

Sarah: I've been thinking about last week's discussion, and I have a question: If we weren't lucky enough to have parents who are humanistic Jews, wouldn't we be just like most of our friends who believe in God? I mean, don't kids just automatically copy their parents' beliefs?

Jon: Most of them do. I have a few friends who agree with me, even though they go to Reform or Conservative temples. But the rest of my friends were brought up to believe in God and they don't question what they were taught.

David: Do *we*? I think Sarah's right. If it weren't for my parents, I would be just like my friends.

Sarah: Then how do we know our beliefs are correct and theirs are wrong? Maybe we're all just "following the leader."

Rabbi: Let's carry the question a step further: Don't Christian kids copy their parents' beliefs, too? How do you know Jews are correct in not believing in Christ? How do we know *anything* is true?

Ken: Just because most people believe what they were taught at home or in school doesn't mean they have to. That's why we have brains—so we can think. Even if my parents believed in God, I'm sure I wouldn't.

David: How can you be sure?

Ken: Because I try to come to my own conclusions about everything. I didn't need my parents to teach me that the idea of God is irrational.

David: Are you saying that the majority of Jews are irrational?

Ken: I'm saying that believing in a "being" who has no shape or form—and therefore no brain—but who created the universe and can think and listen to people's prayers and who cares about what we do on this speck of a planet in a universe so large we can't even measure it—yes, that's irrational, no matter how many people believe it. Just as it is irrational to believe in Christ.

Rabbi:	How do you think you'll raise your kids? Will you raise them as humanists or let them decide for themselves?
Jon:	I'll raise them as humanists. If I don't, they will be like all the other kids. When I was in fourth grade, I told my parents I didn't want to go to Sunday school any more. They said I had to go. That was it. Now I'm glad they didn't allow me to decide for myself.
Sarah:	But they didn't tell you what to believe.
Jon:	They didn't have to. Just sending me to a humanistic Sunday school made me not believe in God.
Sarah:	*Made* you? Not one teacher, not even the rabbi, has ever told us what to believe. Right now, we're free to change our minds and start praying, aren't we?
Rabbi:	What about you, Ken—how will you raise your children?
Ken:	I'll raise them to think for themselves. I'll make it clear to them where I stand and why, but I won't force them to agree with me.
David:	Don't you think that's unrealistic? Kids imitate their parents. If they know you don't believe in God, do you really expect them to disagree?
Ken:	My parents and I disagree about lots of things. We don't like the same music. They are strong Democrats and I'm a Libertarian. But they respect my right to decide for myself, and that's how I'll raise my kids.
Sarah:	What if they want to become Christians. Will you let them?

Ken: How could I stop them? Actually, one of my uncles con-
            verted to Christianity a few years ago. The rest of the family
            practically disowned him. But I admire him for making his
            own decision, even though I think it's irrational.

David: So you won't mind if your kids are irrational?

Ken: Sure I'll mind, but they have to live their own lives. Isn't
            that one of the fundamental principles of Humanistic
            Judaism?* No one—including your parents—can tell you
            what to believe or how to live. I hope that my example will
            help them come to the "right" decision, but it's more
            important that they do their own thinking than that they
            agree with me.

David: I think parents have to teach their children what to
            believe. You wouldn't let your children decide whether
            they can play with matches or take drugs, would you? I
            don't want my kids to believe in God or to even think of
            becoming Christians. It will be my responsibility, as a good
            parent, to give my children the benefit of my thinking and
            experience. Later, when they are adults, they can change
            their minds, but as kids they need to be guided.

Sarah: Isn't there a big difference between taking drugs and
            believing in God? I think you have to control your kids'
            behavior—if it's dangerous or unhealthy—but their beliefs
            should be up to them.

Ken: That's right. If you don't allow them to choose their beliefs,
            how will they ever learn to think for themselves?

---

*Humanistic Judaism is a nontheistic religion that combines a humanistic philosophy of life
with the holidays, symbols, and ceremonies of Jewish culture. Its principles affirm the value of
reason, individual responsibility, and freedom. It interprets Jewish history as the product of human
decisions and actions rather than the unfolding of a divine plan.

Rabbi: I hope you all appreciate the fact that you have already given more thought to what you believe than do many adults much older than you. One of the benefits of being different from the majority is that you are required to be more aware of the reasons for your beliefs. Your convictions are constantly being tested, and, as a result, you may find that your beliefs are more secure than others'. In this respect, not believing in God may make you a stronger person than you otherwise would have been.

CONVERSATION EIGHT

A Rabbis' Roundtable

Rabbi
Conserv(ative):   I was very disturbed by your comment about inter-marriage.

Rabbi
Human(istic):   That it is a natural result of the unprecedented freedom and opportunity that Jews enjoy in America?

Rabbi Conserv: No, I agree with your analysis of the *cause* of the alarming increase in intermarriage in the past few decades. What disturbs me is your willingness to accept this state of affairs and to do nothing to stem the tide of intermarriage, which threatens the very survival of Judaism.

Rabbi Human: Do we have a choice?

Rabbi Conserv: We can fight against intermarriage. We can refuse to officiate at interfaith marriage ceremonies. We can make it clear that under no circumstances will we accept inter-marrieds into our synagogues and temples. We can teach our young people that the future of our people and reli-gion is on their shoulders—that is, in their hearts—and that if they care at all about that future, they must choose mates from within our community.

Rabbi Ref(orm): I have to agree with my Conservative colleague, to a certain extent. If we rabbis indicate that it's okay to marry outside the faith, there will be nothing to stop it. As it is, we may be fighting a losing battle, but at least the community is aware that their leaders disapprove of intermarriage and that may have some effect.

Rabbi Human: You said that you agree "to some extent."

Rabbi Ref: I make it clear to my congregation that I disapprove of intermarriage. I often preach on the subject, and I warn against allowing the prevalence of intermarriage to delude us into thinking it's okay. But once a couple marries, I realize that it's too late to fight against their decision. It's better to accept the couple than to risk alienating the Jewish partner by excluding them from the synagogue and community.

Rabbi Orth(odox): Am I hearing correctly? That you accept non-Jews into your synagogue as members?

Rabbi Ref: Until five years ago, we didn't. But when we found that most of our marriages were intermarriages . . .

Rabbi Orth: Most?

Rabbi Ref: Yes, it's now the minority of marriages where both partners are Jewish. Most of our board of directors have intermarried children. Some of our Sunday school teachers are intermarried. Most of the young couples who apply for membership are intermarried. We realized that our very existence as a congregation is at stake: either we accept these families, or we will be out of business.

Rabbi Orth: Your standard is numbers? Finances? Your temple is a business? What happened to Jewish law? What sort of Judaism will be left when half of your congregation are not even Jewish?

Rabbi Ref: We have created intensive programs to try to attract the non-Jewish spouse to Judaism and to make sure that at least the children are raised as Jews.

Rabbi Orth: If the mother is not Jewish, the children are not,* notwithstanding your "intensive programs."

Rabbi Ref: We accept the Jewishness of the children if *one* parent—mother or father—is Jewish and if the children are raised as Jews.

Rabbi Orth: I'm confused. What can you possibly mean by "Jewish," by "raised as Jews," by "Judaism" if you are so willing to change what all of these words mean as soon as your bank balance drops?

Rabbi Ref: Our purpose is not to support a budget. We're concerned about the survival of Judaism. If we don't adapt to the conditions of modern life, there will be no Jews or Judaism in a hundred years. This has always been the philosophy of Reform Judaism. Change is the law of life.

Rabbi Conserv: I agree with Rabbi Orth. We cannot bend the meaning of Judaism to the point that it is no longer Judaism. Survival at any cost is not what Judaism has ever meant. It is admirable that Reform Judaism is flexible enough to allow for necessary changes when circumstances require them, but it goes too far when the

---

*Halachic Judaism asserts that Jewish identity is transmitted through the mother (although the Bible determines a child's identity through the father).

definition of who is Jewish is changed and, surely, when rabbis not only welcome interfaith families but officiate at their marriage ceremonies!

Rabbi Ref:　　Most Reform rabbis, including me, do not officiate at weddings unless both partners are Jewish.

Rabbi Conserv:　Some do, though. Is there no authority within Reform Judaism that prevents them from doing so?

Rabbi Ref:　　We Reform rabbis may disagree with one another, but we believe each of us has the right to interpret Judaism and to practice it according to his own understanding.

Rabbi Human:　Our respective positions are clear. Rabbi Orth wants a Judaism that is fixed for all time. Rabbi Conserv accepts change within certain boundaries. And Rabbi Ref believes that so long as the ultimate objective is the survival of Judaism, change is legitimate.

Suppose we have entered a new era, which has rendered Judaism obsolete. The ancient beliefs and practices of Halachic Judaism, which are of ultimate importance to Orthodox Judaism, are not embraced by more than a tiny minority of Jews today. Within the Conservative community, the *halacha* is observed by rabbis but the lay population is notoriously lax. Reform Jews barely pay lip service to what, by any standard, can be considered authentic Jewish belief and observance. Intermarriage is but a symptom of a deeper and more significant problem: the lack of interest, not to mention commitment, of the vast majority of contemporary Jews in the Judaism that you wish to promote. Jews are willing to marry non-Jews because they see little difference between themselves and others in terms of their basic values, philosophy of life, and lifestyle. Whereas such differences once were so significant that it would

not have occurred to most Jews to consider marrying
outside the community; today—

Rabbi Orth: Until quite recently, Jews had no choice. The non-
Jewish world would not allow us to marry outsiders.

Rabbi Human: True. We were ostracized. We were a reviled people.
We were locked into insular communities and forced to
maintain a separate existence. Is that the kind of world
to which you would return?

Rabbi Orth.:   Of course not. I appreciate our freedom as much as you
do. But it need not be incompatible with Judaism. Why
do you insist that Judaism is obsolete?

Rabbi Human: Judaism was the creation of a people who experienced
themselves in exile. They responded to centuries of
hostility and exclusion by making a virtue of necessity:
they withdrew into their isolation, immersed themselves in what to them was a sacred system of belief and
practice, and persuaded themselves that theirs was a
superior way of life. They interpreted their isolation
from other peoples as a blessing. It was, they believed,
divinely ordained, as were the myriad of rules and reg-
ulations that reinforced their insularity, including the
prohibition against intermarriage.

Rabbi Orth: You speak as though Jewish law did not issue from God
but came out of the historical situation of the Jewish
people.

Rabbi Human: That is precisely what I mean to say; and now that, for-
tunately, history has truly blessed us with a radically
different world, instead of agonizing over what we have
lost, we may celebrate what we have gained.

Rabbi Conserv: I shall not celebrate the end of Judaism. I shall not dis-
                card what my ancestors fought and died to preserve.

Rabbi Ref: Nor will I.

Rabbi Human: What is it that you wish to preserve?

Rabbi Ref: Our belief in God and His commandments.

Rabbi Human: These are the very matters that are in question. The
                fact is that for many Jewish people, Judaism no longer
                means "belief in God and His commandments."
                Judaism means, at most, an ethnic or cultural inheri-
                tance consisting of a few charming "traditions" that
                engage their interest occasionally—traditions such as
                Chanukah candles and a Passover seder. These sur-
                viving customs are utilized to express their Jewish
                ethnic identity but are not considered divinely
                ordained commandments. If they were so considered,
                we would not be having this discussion.

Rabbi Conserv: We are discussing whether or not Judaism is obsolete.
                You concede that Jewish ethnicity still motivates Jews
                to maintain certain traditions. Can we not capitalize
                on that motivation and encourage more, not less,
                observance? Should we not exploit that ethnicity to
                lead our people back to their *religious* heritage?

Rabbi Human: It is clear that even Jewish ethnicity is in rapid
                decline—if by ethnicity we mean a sense of social or
                cultural distinctiveness. It has all but vanished. The
                very conditions that brought forth the Jewish *religious*
                response—isolation and exclusion from the larger
                society—brought forth the sense of ethnic distinctive-
                ness.

Rabbi Orth: You are asserting that anti-Semitism created both Judaism and Jewishness.

Rabbi Human: I am. Furthermore, as anti-Semitism recedes from the lives of virtually all American Jews—how many of us experience the rejection and victimization that were the daily lot of previous generations?—the reality of social and cultural distinctiveness will continue to decline and will eventually disappear. In another generation or two—barring an unlikely resurgence of discrimination, which would revive Jewish ethnic awareness—even the current weak sense of ethnicity will have faded away, and with it, the vestiges of Jewish identity that persist today.

Rabbi Conserv: And you welcome this? You celebrate the end of Jewishness?

Rabbi Human: I celebrate the end of anti-Semitism. The end of exclusion. The end of over two thousand years of suffering.

Rabbi Ref: Isn't it possible that a new kind of Jewishness will take the place of the old response-to-anti-Semitism Jewishness?

Rabbi Human: I do not deny that an utterly new kind of Jewish identity—a sense of difference not rooted in exclusion—may emerge. However, there is no precedent for such an identity in all of Jewish history, and therefore, no reason to assume that it will arise.

Rabbi Conserv: You are overlooking the Golden Age in Spain,* as well as many periods when Jews enjoyed great vitality and creativity—and Jewish identity flourished.

---

*Tenth to twelfth centuries, under Moslem rule.

Rabbi Human: Yes, there have been periods when, thanks to the *temporary permission* granted to Jews by governmental authorities, they prospered and enjoyed benign treatment. They retained their sense of distinctiveness, however, due to the persistence of the anti-Semitism that excluded them and set them apart from the larger society. The experience of the Jews in America is unique: never before has a country guaranteed, by constitutional law, the absolute and permanent equality and individual rights of its citizens, Jews included.

Rabbi Orth: What constitutions and laws giveth may be taken away. Even America could turn against the Jews.

Rabbi Human: Anything is possible, but the likelihood of what you are suggesting is more remote than my premise: that our good fortune here will continue and that anti-Semitism will continue to decline, leaving us increasingly free to lose our distinctiveness.

Rabbi Ref: If you are correct about our good fortune continuing, why will Jews necessarily lose their motivation to remain Jewish?

Rabbi Human: Once the two-millennia-old consciousness of difference—based upon exclusion—has disappeared, whether future generations of Jews will choose even to draw together into communities of fellow Jews is doubtful. That they will need or wish to formalize and express their Jewishness by means of holidays, ceremonies, and rituals is unlikely. Jewishness will be more a fading memory of ethnic ancestry than an experienced reality.

Rabbi Ref: It saddens me to conceive of the future you predict. Granted, I want us for us a free and happy future. But think of what we would be losing in the process. Do you celebrate the end of Jewish values?

Rabbi Human: I am unaware of distinctive "Jewish values." The values I cherish—such as individual freedom and the right to live one's life without interference from political or religious authority—are the legacy of the Enlightenment rather than the Torah. We Jews are among the most fortunate beneficiaries of that legacy.

Rabbi Ref: I had in mind such values as education, family closeness, concern for one's fellow human beings, charity . . .

Rabbi Human: Whatever values you and I cherish, their validity derives not from who may originally have discovered them—Jew, Greek, or German—but from their effectiveness in promoting human happiness.

Rabbi Orth: I appreciate your honesty. As for me, truth is the highest value, and the Torah is the only reliable source of truth. I cannot give up that source or the authority who gave it to us.

Rabbi Conserv: I became a rabbi in order to teach Judaism. My job is to make it so attractive to observe Shabbat, to keep kosher, to live as Jewish a life as possible, that my people will not even consider giving up their Judaism, much less marry out of the faith.

Rabbi Ref: I feel like the outside here. No, I can't say that all truth is in the Torah, nor can I say that there is no such thing as Jewish values. I became a rabbi to inspire my people to live good lives *and* to live good Jewish lives. Notwithstanding Rabbi Human's declaration that Judaism is obsolete, I still think it is possible to be free *and* practice Judaism. If I didn't, I would not remain a rabbi.

Rabbi Human: History will determine which of us has the most accurate understanding of the Jewish future. I prefer to engage not in fantasies about what Jews should believe and how they should behave, but in a realistic assessment of why they are who they are and what their actual needs and beliefs are. Rather than blame them for being disloyal to standards created in different times and places, I prefer to encourage them to create standards appropriate to our time and place and to live with integrity according to those standards.

SUMMARY

*Seven
~~Commandments~~
Suggestions for the
Twenty-First Century*

1. Accept "yes" for an answer. The news is good. Anti-Semitism, the bane of Jewish existence for twenty centuries, has virtually disappeared. Jews are no longer outsiders. They are not persecuted victims. No constraints inhibit their choices, occupational or personal. They are among the most successful, influential, creative, and affluent achievers in American history and society. Appreciate this good fortune. Celebrate the unprecedented freedom and opportunity that Jews enjoy in this century.

2. Do not worry about the survival of the Jews. Thirty centuries of persecution, exclusion, and deprivation did not destroy them. If freedom, equality, and opportunity cause their assimilation, it is a small price to pay for the happiness and dignity that past generations could only pray for.

3. Do not weep if your child intermarries. That she or he is free to do so is a sign of the acceptance and liberties that Jews now enjoy. Inasmuch as being Jewish no longer carries disabilities, there is a good chance that your child's partner will want to be Jewish, too, or will at least want the children to be. In any event, be grateful that it is at last possible to marry the person one loves, without regard to anachronistic and irrelevant religious and ethnic labels.

4. Be honest about your beliefs. Do not pretend to believe what you in fact do not believe. Your beliefs should never be a source of guilt. It is

105

okay, for example, not to believe in God. Many Jews do not. They and you have the right to decide what to believe regardless of what authorities in the past or present say. Realize that the beliefs of ancient Jews were their response to reality as they experienced it. Yours will likely be different, inasmuch as your experience is different. The Judaism that was created by people who found themselves in exile, as helpless victims, as an ostracized and reviled people, will not be meaningful or satisfying to you.

5. Do not try to prove that you are Jewish. If you want to be, you are. There are as many definitions of, and ways to be, a Jew as there are Jews. Some are religious; some are not. No way is better than another. Only you can decide what being Jewish means to you.

6. Realize that, whatever your theology, you are a spiritual person. Unless you have no use for music or literature or art. Unless you are oblivious to the genius of Shakespeare and Chopin. Unless you are indifferent to the majesty of a mountain range or the spectacle of a starry sky. Your spirituality comes entirely from within you. That is your greatness.

7. Share in the new Jewish Emancipation. The first Emancipation in the eighteenth and nineteenth centuries was political. It granted Jews the right to participate as equals in the political, economic, and social life of the larger society. The second Emancipation is the twenty-first century's. It is psychological and spiritual. It frees our minds and hearts from the beliefs of the past so that we may think new thoughts and create new convictions. We cannot know where the new Emancipation will take us. Knowing from whence we came, though, we can be sure it is a blessing.

Five Postreligious Spiritual Truths

(As Suggested by a Reading
of the Book of Job)

1.   Contrary to sentimentalists, nature is not kind, generous, or even beautiful. These are qualities that humanity imposes upon nature, which is uncaring, insensitive, and oblivious to morality. Neither prayer nor virtue has any effect whatsoever upon floods or earthquakes. Good people are swept away with the wicked. Just as you may unwittingly squash a bug under your heel as you cross the street, so do rocks and water, without design, consign to death countless human beings of all ages, races, and religions. Nature is blind to our purposes and needs. This is reality, and no religious platitude will change it. We may call a sunset beautiful or a mountain grand, but these are not qualities that inhere in nature. They exist entirely in the eyes of their human beholders.

2.   Life is not fair. We do not get what we deserve. The good sometimes die young. The evil sometimes prosper. It is a waste of time and energy to wonder, "Why me?" when afflicted by whatever natural calamity. What we can do is to use our imagination, our reason, and our experience to discover ways to improve the conditions of human life, to help one another, and to minimize the suffering that we can control. Death is real. No one can escape it. When we are wise, we realize that, were it not for death, life would be cheap and meaningless. There would always be another day to do what one still has failed to do, to love, to learn. Thus,

107

doing, loving, learning would be for no purpose. Death makes life the most precious of all commodities because it is ineluctable, because it is final.

3.   If there is to be any justice at all in the world, it is only because we create it. Justice is not handed down from on high. It is a purely human invention. All moral responsibility in the world comes from us human beings. All moral values, all standards of right and wrong, good and evil are created by human beings. Which is not to say that they are not real. Love is real. Compassion is real. Dignity and justice are as real as flesh and bones. But they are not qualities "out there." They are, as far as we know, only in us among all living things.

4.   Not being gods, we are fallible. No human who has ever lived can be certain that he or she knows *the* truth. One may be pretty sure, but never entirely sure. And "pretty" is a long way from "entirely." So we must live with a built-in humility factor that keeps us from imposing our maybe-truth on those who disagree with us. Most of the misery caused by human beings is due to the folly of presumptuousness: assuming that my truth must be yours and forcing you to accept it. Most of the happiness created by human beings is due to allowing each person to live by his or her own light.

5.   While there are more powerful forces in the universe than we (the forces of wind, water, fire, and the inexorable march of time), and while these amoral forces of nature may ultimately destroy us physically, no nonhuman power can rob us of our personal dignity. As the only value-creating and value-preserving beings in existence, we fulfill our destiny as humans by honoring our noblest aspirations. Even death is powerless to erase the memory of our existence.